Marriage God's Way

Copyright © 2018 by Shiloh Ministries, Inc.

ISBN 978-0-9890789-6-2

Published by Shiloh Ministries, Inc., in July, 2018

> Scripture quotations marked "ESV" are taken from *The Holy Bible, English Standard Version*. Copyright © 2000, 2001 by Crossway Bibles, a division of Good News Publishers. Used by permission. All rights reserved.
>
> Scripture quotations marked "KJV" are taken from *The King James Version of the Holy Bible*, public domain.
>
> Scripture quotations marked *"The Message"* are taken from *The Message: The Bible in Contemporary English*™. Copyright © 1993, 1994, 1995, 1996, 2000, 2001, 2002. Used by permission of NavPress Publishing Group.
>
> Scripture quotations marked "NIV" are taken from the *Holy Bible, New International Version*®. Copyright © 1973, 1978, 1984 by International Bible Society. Used by permission of Zondervan. All rights reserved.
>
> Scripture quotations marked "NKJV" are taken from the *New King James Version*. Copyright © 1982 by Thomas Nelson, Inc. Used by permission. All rights reserved.
>
> Scripture quotations marked "NLT" are taken from the *Holy Bible, New Living Translation*. Copyright © 1996. Used by permission of Tyndale House Publishers, Inc., Wheaton, IL 60189 USA. All rights reserved.

All rights reserved. This book is protected by the copyright laws of the United States of America, and may not be copied or reprinted for commercial use or profit. No part of this book may be reproduced or transmitted in any form or by any means – electronic, mechanical or photographic – including photocopying, recording or by any information storage and retrieval system, without prior written permission of the publisher. No patent liability is assumed with respect to the use of the information contained herein. The publisher and authors assume no responsibility for errors or omissions; neither is any liability assumed for damages resulting from use of the information contained herein.

Permission is granted to share the principles in this book with individuals, churches and prayer groups. These principles may be used in sermons and Bible studies.

Printed in the United States of America.

MARRIAGE GOD'S WAY

This Book Belongs to

_____

Presented by

_____

Barbara: Age 38	Randy : Age 34
Second marriage, 3 children	Never married
From California	From Northern Virginia
Owned a 5-bedroom house	Owned a 2-bedroom house
Had 1 dog, 1 cat	Had 2 dogs
Artist and sign painter	Newspaper reporter

    We were acquainted for 5 years, then dated 4 months, and were married November 6, 1982. We had 100 people at our wedding. It cost around $100. We had a covered dish reception in Barbara's house. Her ex in-laws watched the children while we honeymooned in Washington, D.C.

    Our Sunday school teacher came to the wedding because the Lord told him to tell us, "This is of Me, but it's going to be hard, hard, hard." It was a true prophecy. It was hard, hard, hard.

Contents

	Introduction	IV
Chapter 1	It Wasn't Easy	1
Chapter 2	Intergenerational Healing	6
Chapter 3	The Mirror Image Principle	11
Chapter 4	The Double-minded Man vs. Agreement	14
Chapter 5	Unfaithfulness	21
Chapter 6	Emotional Adultery	24
Chapter 7	The Orphan Spirit	30
Chapter 8	Atmosphere for Increase	37
Chapter 9	Where Do You Hurt/Hide?	44
Chapter 10	Disciplining our Emotions	54
Chapter 11	Differences Between Men and Women	63
	Marriage God's Way Brochure	69
	Ordering Books	80

It Wasn't Easy

We have a great marriage – we love us. We have taken many lumps since our wedding in 1982, but now we love each other more and are grateful to spend every day together. We have experienced more fun, productivity and friendship with each other and the Lord than ever before. We affirm our love often throughout the day. We know God brought us together for our good and the advancement of His Kingdom. But it wasn't always like this.

You will see what a mess we were. God uses those who are the most unlikely to succeed as a backdrop for His overcoming power. This is not to say that every marriage will be healed. But in our case, it was.

HOW WE STARTED

Randy: I married my friend Barbara. She was beautiful, a hard worker, smart and talented. And she always had stories of faith. We had been acquainted for five years before the romance started. Then we got married after only four months of dating and just two months after I gave my heart to Jesus.

Barbara: It seemed right to marry Randy, although I'd had a few serious relationships since being divorced. My three children were all from my only other marriage, which lasted 9 years.

I loved Randy's calming voice and his beautiful hands. We enjoyed talking to each other, and still do. But we didn't know each other at all. I had raised my kids by myself for another 9 years, without child support or help from my parents. I worked three, even four jobs at a time to make ends meet.

NIGHTMARE REALITY

Randy: Three days after returning from our honeymoon, I called the clerk of court to see if I could get our marriage annulled because we fought so much when we got home. The clerk said I needed a lawyer. I wasn't working and had no money so I forgot that idea.

I had moved into Barbara's house with all my junk – brown scratchy furniture, four-foot-tall stereo speakers, and two large smelly dogs. All this offended Barbara's sense of style and space. I married Florence Nightingale and came home from the honeymoon with Attila the Hun.

Two months later, Barbara went to Florida to drive her ex-boss's mother back to Maryland. There was no money or food in the house for me and the two children (by then, the oldest had left home for the mission field). I was still not working and not looking for a job.

While Barbara was gone, we survived a hurricane. I wasn't loving at all, and the kids didn't like me. I still lived by my old adage, "If you don't like the way I act, don't let the door hit you on the way out." I didn't respect women very much and had always used them. I was passive-aggressive and Barbara is confrontational. It was a recipe for quarreling.

Barbara: I was successful and generally positive, used to being in control, and a work-a-holic. I was well-known as an artist and sign painter, and I was buying my own house. I sent my three children to Christian school, paid all my bills on time, and was determined to keep my head above water. I was very busy in public ministry, but I also had a rejection complex with bouts of depression and anger, sometimes severe.

I didn't have much respect for men, especially lazy men. I had already been through one divorce and decided not to wait for years if this marriage wasn't going to work.

IF WE CAN MAKE IT, ANYONE CAN MAKE IT

Randy: You can see that we didn't have much to work with at first, except for our faith in God. And with God, all things are possible. It was a pivotal moment when Barbara suggested getting a divorce. I said, "We made a vow before God and we're going to keep it."

Barbara: We were still friends, in spite of the constant bickering. And we were always able to pray together, even in the middle of a big argument. Although I thought of divorce, I still liked Randy as a friend. When we were married, we were two damaged people wrapped in pretty packages, and we didn't know any of the awful stuff inside.

We often say that we're glad we didn't know each other any better before our wedding, or we never would have married. That's how easily we could have missed our destiny.

So many people, young and old, are not getting married anymore but living together. Many older people do it for financial reasons, whereas younger people don't see the need. This includes Christians.

Randy: The marriage relationship is intended to be a reflection of our relationship with our Father in heaven. Both are covenant relationships, not a casual arrangement of convenience. That covenant kept us together.

We asked the Lord which is better, a faithful unmarried couple or an unfaithful married couple? He said, "Remember that marriage is a vow. Taking a vow before God and man is different from agreeing to live together. Not everyone needs a vow to be faithful, but it saved your marriage."

Barbara: My life changed six years before I married Randy. Exhausted from overwork, I threw myself on my bed and declared, "Lord, I'm so tired. I'm ready to do things Your way now. I'm going to read the Bible, believe it and do it."

God is still teaching us the same stuff as in the beginning, when Randy and I had a vision of advancing the Kingdom together. We learned that progress isn't just going forward; it's an upward spiral. Sometimes when we seem to be going over the same place and not making progress, we really are.

Reflections

The Lord told us about Peace...

"When you both have peace, your ministry and marriage will shine so brightly that people will come to you to learn. They will ask your secret, expecting a magic formula. Of course you prayed, but then you had to walk it out. It took time, great effort and sacrifice. You learned to give up judgment and impatience. You learned to outgrow a 'woe is me' spirit which provokes resentment and passivity. You made the effort to get on the same page and you had to sacrifice your selfishness."

Randy: We were still bickering a lot into our third year together, even though we were ministering. When we asked a couple to pray for us, the Lord revealed that a spirit of competition was dividing Barbara and me. We each thought our time and activities were more important, and expected the other to stop and help.

Barbara kept saying we needed to be a team. I liked doing things alone. I thought, if I want something done right I have to do it myself.

Barbara started writing a column called "Things Hoped For" in the *Manna*, a regional Christian newspaper I did for 25 years. Her column became its most popular feature. Her concepts were wonderful, but she didn't know grammar or spelling, and wrote out each installment in pencil – one long paragraph. I complained to the Lord, "No editor in the world should have to review copy like this." He said, "I only made one of you an editor. I gave her other gifts."

As I corrected her grammar, I also changed her writing voice. This really made her angry. She even threatened to move back to California because she was so frustrated with me.

We still write together, and now she even edits me. We make a good team. We've come a long way!

Barbara: When we were told we had a spirit of competition, we looked at each other and said in unison, "We sure do, but Lord, we don't know what to do about it. You'll have to help us." And He did. From that day forward we became less competitive and less selfish, and slowly started becoming a team. We are still learning and overcoming.

The Lord reminded us to bring our issues to Him and ask for wisdom. And as we agree with Him, we naturally agree with each other.

A LIFELONG ADVENTURE

Our friends Matt and Melody Bernatitus are the MD, DC, VA prayer team leaders/directors for FamilyLife's *A Weekend to Remember*. They wrote,

> "Great marriages don't just happen. Marriage is a lifelong adventure of growing together through every age and stage of life. The happiest couples are those who commit to learning skills that help them weather difficult seasons and deal competently with relationship challenges."

Reflections
The Lord told us about Persevering...

"If you're digging for treasure, you have to keep at it until you hit pay dirt. It may take awhile. If you get discouraged along the way, someone has to remind you why you're doing it. So keep the goal in sight. Once you find what you are looking for, it won't matter how much work there was.

"You don't know it while you are getting nearer to your goal until it finally comes into view. While you are digging, there is plenty of time to think, 'Why am I doing this?' But you keep digging just like you keep learning. And you have no way to measure progress until your anticipation is rewarded. You could have given up along the way and let frustration get the better of you, but you persevered because there was a glimmer of hope.

"So don't be discouraged that it seems like you're still learning the same old lessons, still digging the same old hole. Have faith that you are drawing nearer to your goal and that your faithfulness is perfecting you."

Chapter 1 – It Wasn't Easy

PRAY Father, help us persevere in the hard times. Help us give up selfishness and see each other as a gift from You. Help us be faithful to our vows.

Intergenerational Healing

Randy: In our first year of marriage, a visiting pastor at The Son'Spot, a Christian coffeehouse in the nearby Atlantic resort of Ocean City where we ministered, made a passing reference to something called "intergenerational healing." Barbara and I glanced at each other and said in unison that we wanted to know more. He was reluctant because it was long and involved, but we pressed until he consented.

Intergenerational healing is deliverance from patterns of disobedience which recur from generation to generation. It is based on how God described His nature to Moses in Exodus 34:6-7 (ESV)—

"The Lord, the Lord, a God merciful and gracious, slow to anger, and abounding in steadfast love and faithfulness, keeping steadfast love for thousands, forgiving iniquity and transgression and sin, but who will by no means clear the guilty, visiting the iniquity of the fathers on the children and the children's children, to the third and the fourth generation."

In a tiny prayer room, the pastor directed Barbara and me in the steps of deliverance. We each identified weaknesses and areas of our own disobedience which we could see in our parents, such as a predisposition toward immorality, addiction, resentment, self-pity, and a martyr spirit. As we called them out by name, we repented and renounced their works in us. We applied the Blood of Jesus and the Word of God to sever their roots in us, and commanded those roots to wither and die.

It was an intensive process. After we finished, I asked the pastor, "Is it true that when you are set free from something, Satan will try to make you believe nothing happened?"

"Count on it," the pastor replied firmly.

LOOKING FOR SOMEONE TO BLAME

The next day I awoke to the sound of arguing in my head. The voices were mine and Barbara's. For no apparent reason, I was seething with resentment – a fight looking for a place to happen. As we drove back to Ocean City that day,

I waited for something in our conversation to give me an excuse to explode. Without provocation, I suddenly jerked the car onto the grassy median and announced, "I don't have to put up with this! I'll get out and walk!"

Not easily one-upped, Barbara retorted, "Don't bother, I will."

We were both harboring resentment.

Resentment is a passive form of anger. Like lust and jealousy and a host of other emotions, resentment simmers under the surface until it is triggered. An angry person looks for someone else to blame so he doesn't have to look at himself. It seems I had harbored some form of resentment most of my life.

Reflections
The Lord told us about Resentment...

"Resentment always results in accusations. When you are resentful, you think you have resentment toward another person. Resentment is deceitful. The truth is, you just have resentment, and the first person who annoys you becomes your target.

"When you recognize how resentment arrives without a target, it is easier to see it as a spiritual attack against you instead of an offense generated by someone else."

"WHERE DID THAT COME FROM?"

As I watched my wife get out of the car and start walking home, my triumph seemed hollow. Part of me wanted to feel vindicated. The other part asked, "What have you done?" Too proud to hasten and try to correct what happened, I stopped to get gas and let her walk awhile. I thought I was within my rights. After stalling as long as I dared, I drove back and coaxed her into the car.

Somehow, my petty power play had gone terribly wrong. Not one to put up with any form of abuse, Barbara already determined she would move in with her sister in California. As far as she was concerned, our marriage was over.

There was an icy wedge between us when we got home. Hurt and offended, we retreated to different parts of the house. I was alone in our bedroom. Even though self-pity made me feel like a victim, the gravity of what I had done was starting to descend on me. A knot in my stomach told me I was about to face terrible consequences.

"Where did that come from?" I asked God. Maybe I had reacted to the remark someone made to me the previous night, "We all know who wears the pants in *your* family."

But my resentment started long before we were married. Maybe it was due to an unholy vow (an unrighteous commitment which invites demonic influence) I made to myself as an adolescent. I didn't want to be responsible for bringing anyone into the world to be as miserable as I was, so I determined never to have children or get married. I wrote that pledge on a piece of paper and hid it inside a basement wall. I never forgot it.

Reflections

The Lord told us about Anger...

"No matter how you try to justify it, most anger comes from other people not fulfilling your selfish needs.

"'Selfish needs' covers a large area. It can include anything from possessions to respect. Being concerned with Self makes anger a convenient way to get what you want.

"Look at the man who batters his wife. Why is he angry? Because she can't give him what he believes he deserved growing up. No one can. He feels cheated out of security and affirmation and love. The more he tries to make another person his source for these things, the more angry he becomes when his needs are not met. And anger always provokes more anger.

"So how do you overcome anger? How do you learn to be unselfish? How can a wounded person ever give up rights? By learning to love. Even imperfect love can teach these things, but it has to be love and not manipulation.

"If love is just another way to get what you want, it's actually a substitute for anger. But if love truly cares about the other person, generosity of spirit will follow.

"Anger is a form of fear — a response to the thought that your needs won't be met. Love casts out fear, including anger. But it has to be genuine love that thinks about more than getting what it wants."

Chapter 2 – Intergenerational Healing

BAD FRUIT

The fruit of that unholy vow was the two children I fathered and had aborted while I was single. I didn't know an abortion ended the life of a person. In fact, I was glad when *Roe v. Wade* paved the way for legalized abortion. If I got someone pregnant, I thought, I could destroy the evidence so I wouldn't have to take responsibility.

I bought into the amoral belief that abortion was somehow merciful. I knew young couples who were pressured into marrying for the sake of their unborn child, only to lead despondent and spiteful lives. I asked myself, "Were they better off? Were their children?"

After I was born into God's family, I comprehended how selfish abortion is. I also recognized that women bear the brunt of guilt for it. The men who impregnate them, and often insist on and pay for their abortions, seldom assume the blame for ending a life.

I went from celebrating abortion to lamenting my participation in it. I begged God's forgiveness. It was a part of my old life that I asked Him to pardon when I went to the altar and cried out, "My heart is so black!" I think it was easier for God to forgive me than for me to forgive myself.

Although in my youth I had resolved to remain single and never to become a parent, now I had taken a wife who had three children. The things I said I wouldn't do were fueling my resentment.

Reflections

The Lord told us about Trials...

"If the enemy can get you to side with him and accuse God, you will never see the good in a trial. Trials don't advance you unless you recognize good coming out of them. If you don't receive a benefit, all you have left is a trial.

"You recognize God's faithfulness when you see the good coming out of a trial. Satan wants to obscure God's faithfulness from you, because that provides grounds for an accusation against God.

"Satan works very hard to get your eyes off of the Creator and onto the creation so you will complain, and then conclude you are better off doing it by yourself. That's why Paul wrote that no trial or lack can separate us from the love of God.

"Nothing can come between you and God's faithfulness, not even deception, unless you allow it."

PRAY Father, forgive us for receiving and perpetuating the iniquities that have come down to us through our blood line. Forgive us for blaming others and even You. Help us take responsibility for our own actions.

Forgive us for resentment and anger brought on by trying to control other people and circumstances. Forgive us for not trusting You to be our Loving Father who has our best interests at heart. Teach us to trust You more as You bring all things around for good.

The Mirror Image Principle

Randy: Back at home, after our big fight in the car, I talked to God as though I were the injured party. I waited for Him to tell me what Barbara did to set me off, but He would not play my game. Instead, He spoke a revolutionary truth which we now call the Mirror Image Principle:

> "Your relationship with your wife is a mirror image of your relationship with Me. So if you're having problems, don't look at her. Look at yourself. Get your relationship right with Me and I'll take care of the woman."

That was so far from what I expected, it had to be God. But wait a minute. He was saying it was my fault. He reminded me that, as the head of my household, I am accountable for everything that happens under my roof, even if I'm not directly responsible for it. That is God's chain of command.

I had never assumed the place of headship or authority in my home. I expected Barbara to do all the spiritual heavy lifting, then I became resentful when I felt disrespected. I was supposed to be leading the formation but had been trying to hide in the ranks.

Still looking for justification, I demanded, "But did You see what she did?"

I was hoping there was a loophole. I thought there had to be special consideration for someone like me. That's when God got tough.

"Okay, here's what you're going to do. From now on, you're not allowed to have another critical thought about your wife or say another unkind word to her. You keep your nose in the Word and your mind in prayer and get your relationship right with Me, and let Me take care of her."

I wanted the Lord to side with me, but He didn't side with anyone. As His words echoed in my head, I began to realize that I was holding back in my marriage. I didn't want to make that last bit of emotional commitment because I didn't fully trust Barbara to have my best interest at heart. This was a reflection of my attitude toward God. The same mistrust which hindered our marriage was keeping me from true intimacy with God, the Lover of my Soul. Whether it was due to fear or selfishness didn't matter. It was an impediment – a strategic barrier which obstructed all my relationships.

Rather than placing a burden on me, God's revelation was liberating. It was an extension of the intergenerational healing that started the night before.

Reflections

The Lord told us about Being the Head...

"When you pray for humility, you pray to be abased. I have made you a humble man of God. Prove it. Stop thinking about yourself so much and think about others. Don't only think about their needs but their convenience. Don't make your wife the last one you have charity toward. Your wife should be first.

"This is not only for you, but you have to lead in it. I'll strengthen you, but you must perform it. Be Christ in your home. Being a head is not only a position, it is a responsibility. The head receives honor not because of his position but because of his thoughtfulness."

I'd had a supernatural encounter with God. When I found Barbara to tell her what happened, she wasn't impressed. She was still thinking about going to California, not looking for reconciliation.

Our house was a mausoleum, no longer alive with the usual activity and conversation. Barbara and I were like mannequins, void of emotion or any remembrance of joy. Even so, I could not let myself be distracted from the assignment God gave me. I had to stay focused on getting my relationship right with Him.

"Let Me take care of her," reminded a quiet inner voice.

Work and ministry – which once seemed paramount to me – were no longer as important. In the days that followed, it wasn't so much *what* I learned from reading the Word; it was the *discipline* of trusting and submitting to God that changed things. I prayed. I asked all of our friends to pray for us. I could no longer afford to play the victim. I had to humble myself.

Chapter 3 – The Mirror Image Principle

Barbara's plans to move west never materialized. At the end of the first week, she came to me and said hesitantly, "I *want* to be in love with you again." I knew I had to keep trusting God to take care of her. I maintained my regimen of Bible reading and prayer.

After two weeks the tension broke. Each of us possessed a much deeper tenderness and appreciation for the other. My old resentments gave way to new freedom as I determined to trust God and my wife with a full measure of devotion.

We were more in love than ever. It was as though our life together had been born all over again. As our relationship continued to improve, God showed us other principles which eventually formed our teaching on marriage.

God brought our partnership from despair to spiritual prosperity. It was all pretty amazing to me as I reflected on our backgrounds. Before we were wed, Barbara as a single mother had trouble trusting men. I had not been previously married and was terminally selfish. How does God combine two broken vessels like us and make something beautiful?

I asked Him that one day as I considered His grace to us, and He replied,

> "Most married people seek me individually, but you and Barbara have always prayed together. You have a one-flesh relationship with Me."

The Mirror Image Principle has become the heart of our teaching on marriage: *"Your relationship with your spouse is a mirror image of your relationship with Me."*

I was too much in love with Jesus to break a covenant. He gave me back my life that I had wasted. Before I became a Christian, I was unwilling to give my whole self to anything but me. I would only give a portion.

A covenant is a promise that allows no excuses. It is holy. All covenants are as unto God, and breaking them incurs a great risk. It is better to surrender your life than to break a covenant. If you enter a covenant and you're not committed, you won't keep it.

PRAY Father, I have disobeyed Your Word by not loving others and my spouse as I love myself. I have made my interests and desires more important than theirs. I see that as I treat others, that is how I'm treating You. Help me reflect Your love and forgive me for not treating others the way I would like to be treated.

The Double-minded Man vs. Agreement

Randy: For the first 20 years of our marriage, Barbara and I were always together. We were privileged to have so much time to talk and pray, to work on projects and ministry. I had trouble understanding why she kept saying we needed to become more of a team.

Whenever we came into conflict, my way of handling it was to be passive and try to ignore it. Barbara's was to meet it head-on, sometimes without thinking things through. The difference in the way we approached problems added to the friction, but I couldn't see it as a lack of teamwork.

I said to myself, "We're husband and wife. We do everything together. How much more of a team can we be?" I thought her veiled meaning was that I didn't do everything her way.

Even though it wasn't a major bone of contention, we always seemed to return to it. This went on for years. Barbara prayed that God would help me see what she meant by teamwork.

One day I was waiting in the car for her to return from a store. I was probably listening to the radio – not doing anything spiritual. That's how I knew it was God when, over top of whatever I was thinking, I heard a question in my head: **"What does My Word say about the double-minded man?"**

Immediately my spirit came to attention. I recognized this as a pop quiz and I wanted to pass it. I thought I had an advantage because I remembered the passage in James which says the double-minded man is like a wave tossed on the sea, unstable in all his ways, and should not expect to receive anything from God. I recited the answer, but God was about to reveal its meaning.

Next I heard, "You know I see you and Barbara as one flesh, right?"

> "That means, since you're one flesh, that whenever you disagree, you're just like the double-minded man."

Chapter 4 – The Double-minded Man vs. Agreement

In other words, anytime we weren't in one accord, we were like a wave tossed on the sea, unstable in all our ways, and should not expect to receive anything from God. It took a minute to sink in.

I wanted to find a loophole so I asked, "You mean if we are working on something and we disagree, and three days later we are working on something else, You won't help us with the second thing until we agree on the first?"

The Lord replied, *"You got it!"* I finally recognized the importance of what Barbara had been telling me all this time. The message couldn't be any plainer. To be a team, we had to work at being in agreement.

Reflections
The Lord told us about Double-mindedness...

"You can pray and then worry and cancel the effectiveness of your prayer. That's the true definition of double-mindedness.

"Part of faith is not preparing for failure. Whenever you make contingency plans, you are watering seeds of doubt and giving Satan a legal right to cause you to fail. You do that to protect your emotions so as not to be so disappointed."

THE ONE WITH THE GIFT

When I told Barbara what God said, we were both very excited. We began to see ourselves as a ship. As the one usually gifted with vision, Barbara is the sails. I'm the anchor which keeps us stable. If we are always at full sail, we will blow off course. And if we don't weigh anchor and get underway, we'll never go anywhere. We have to work together.

The Lord helped by teaching us that the one with greater wisdom in a given situation is the one He holds more accountable. He also taught us to *"defer to the one who has the gift."*

When we were first married, Barbara wanted to repaint the exterior of our house. She asked me to select the colors. Big mistake. She is the artist. She knows what colors go together and look best. I don't. I picked what appealed to me – a gaudy gold for the exterior and a dark chocolate for the shutters and trim. She hated it. The kids hated it. Barbara was honoring me by letting me choose. Her intentions were better than my judgment.

Reflections

The Lord told us about Becoming One...

"No process was necessary for Jesus and Me to be totally One because He came from Me.

"Couples come from different places and form a union; so for them, becoming one is a process of yielding to each other.

"Included in that process is recognizing gifted areas in one another and learning to trust. That's when the two together become greater than the two separately. It's really a process of humility. Those who are willing will find great joy in it.

"Working together is one thing and accomplishing things together is another. Here's what you should be learning. Your differences make you stronger because you each have unique giftings. If you value them, they will unite you. Don't let them divide you.

"When men are insecure, they are double-minded. So I wait for them to become more desperate. Love is a good reason for men to come to Me, but desperation will do in a pinch."

By the time we were building our new house, I had learned not to assert my taste in areas where I'm not gifted. When Barbara asked what color to paint one of the rooms, I replied, "I really don't have a preference. I'd like you to choose." I wasn't being passive. I was surrendering the right to an opinion so we could take advantage of her gift. We were finally starting to become a team.

There are times when it's more important to be in agreement than to be correct. The Lord told us, "Don't you know I can build empires out of your mistakes?"

FIRE DRILLS

Once we were on the same page concerning teamwork, our prayer life shifted again. Evening devotions became spiritual strategy sessions. The power of agreement so captured us that we were like children with a new toy. We thought about every area where we might not agree, compared our preferences, and prayed to come into one accord if we didn't see eye-to-eye. We weren't picking fights, we were working at being single-minded.

We started calling these sessions "fire drills" because we wanted to identify potential dangers and create avenues of escape. This was hard work.

It helped me progress from being passive-resentful to valuing the emotional maturity and spiritual strength of teamwork. We studied and discussed the book of James daily for six months, especially the first chapter.

AGREEMENT

Barbara: Agreement is so important. Remember the Tower of Babel? The Lord said that because the people were in one accord as they built a tower that reached to heaven, nothing would be impossible for them. So He confused their language and they could no longer communicate and be in agreement. The place was named Babel (Genesis 11:1-8).

Once, Randy and I were incorrectly described in a local newspaper which said, "They agree to disagree." This is not true. We try not to do anything unless we come into agreement. It takes work to come into agreement. Sometimes we don't even know if we agree or not until we confront an issue. The Lord taught us that it is hard to hear Him when we have our own opinions. Once we have both spoken our opinion, then we can go to the Lord and let Him direct our thinking. If we are not sure, we wait.

> "To be a successful team, you must have shared vision, shared responsibility and shared workload. Competition undermines your vision. When important issues have to be decided by who is right, conflict can't be far behind."

Reflections
The Lord told us about Being Positive...

"Being positive at your center will dislodge fear. You can't be double-minded about it. If you're not all positive, the leaven of negativity will cause it not to work. Being positive is more than a confession, it's a state of the heart, out of which flow the issues of life.

"Being positive is simply agreeing with Me. Being negative is agreeing with the world. When things you see and hear around you instinctively make you draw back, it's because they are attacking the positive. The older you get, the more you withdraw from the world, not because you want to be in heaven right away but because you want heaven to be in you while you're still here.

"With wisdom, influence and favor, you can get more done than with hard work, *if you trust Me.*"

Reflections

The Lord told us about Teamwork...

"Daughter, you can't expect your husband to be as observant as you are. It's not in his hormones and not in his nature. You should not expect him to operate in your gifts anymore than you should operate in his.

"Getting annoyed with him because he doesn't see what you see is not the spirit of teamwork. You are on duty for both of you. You both see and know different things, and that's what makes you a great team.

"You cannot make your husband do the right thing. And even if he does, you can't force him to have a right attitude. Your energy would be far better spent lifting him up to Me and letting My Spirit examine his heart and teach him what is right. Then he will do the right thing for the right reason.

"Son, don't question your wife's motives. She wants your well-being, just as I do. And what you sometimes consider disrespectful is simply expedient to her. If you don't take offense, you won't give offense. This is the next rung of the teamwork ladder.

"What you do, do joyfully. If My Kingdom is righteousness, peace and joy, why do you go about its business feeling bad about yourself, and suspicious of others and each other?

"Becoming a better team will always be new because you continue to improve. Do not dismiss or misjudge the past. It's not just knowing where you are but where you've come from. Assess the progress you two have made in your teamwork. Do you know what facilitated it? Learning to trust each other more.

"In your relationship, you lack full understanding of how to trust. You are looking for a guarantee that your spouse will get something right before you concede to trust. There are no guarantees.

"You need to learn to trust one another's intentions. Let Me take care of the outcomes, and remember that they will be better if you are in agreement."

Randy: The Lord once told us, "I would rather you two oppose Me than each other because I can take it, but you can't." Obviously we don't want to be on the other side from the Lord on any issue. He was telling us how important it is for Barbara and me not to oppose each other. That is being double-minded.

We have made some bad decisions over the years. Some caused us to suffer loss. But because we decided together, we could not blame each other and we learned from our mistakes. The prophet Amos wrote, **"Can two walk together, except they be agreed?"** (Amos 3:3 KJV).

It is possible to share the workload without sharing the responsibility. When Barbara said, "We haven't been a team," the Lord responded,

Reflections
The Lord told us about Not Being a Team...

"Saying you've never been a team dishonors what I've done. Of course there is room for improvement, and you are improving because it's human nature to keep doing something you are good at.

"When you overreact, it's because you're afraid you won't be heard. When you fear, it's because you're afraid your needs won't be met. This sets you up to argue and accuse and feel alone. Does that sound like the enemy dividing you? That means that you are letting the enemy direct the conversation.

"No one can take your teamwork away from you – past or present. Don't dishonor it, even as you work to make it better. You have the potential to become such a 'one flesh' that you won't even need to tell each other what must be done.

"Becoming one flesh is the result of common goals – shared vision, shared workload, shared responsibility. See how far you've come, not how far you have to go, and you will be more grateful to Me for each other."

Reflections

The Lord told us about Anger and Blaming...

"When you dwell on the conflicts, you forget the 95 percent of the time that you do work well together. When you dwell on the five percent, it seems like more of a problem than it really is.

"When you have your occasional clash over who gets to be in charge, don't take it to heart. You know the enemy wants to amplify differences into a crisis.

"Learn to combine your resources and styles more all the time. Learn to adapt rather than correct each other's sense of order. If you take more time and you respect rather than correct one another, you'll have more to work with.

"Drop all pretense of anger and blaming. Your number one assignment is to not let yourself be divided. Your number two assignment is to trust Me to use all these things for good. If you do those, you'll automatically complete your number three assignment, which is to hold your peace.

"Work on peace in the little things until you have peace in everything."

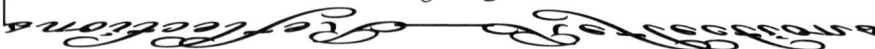

PRAY Lord, please help my spouse and me see ourselves as one flesh. Help us not be double-minded so we will prosper in our marriage and in every aspect of our lives. Forgive us for being lazy and not working harder at our marriage, and help us do the work of coming into agreement.

Unfaithfulness

"Every good and perfect gift is from above, coming down from the Father of the heavenly lights..."(James 1:17 NIV).

Randy: The Lord gives me pop quizzes to help me overcome my weak areas. Once when I was complaining to Him about Barbara, He responded,

> "Your wife is My good and perfect gift to you, and she is sufficient for all your needs. Therefore, whenever you complain about her, you are complaining against Me."

He reminded me that He used Barbara to love my unsaved soul and bring me into His Kingdom. She was the good and perfect gift who helped me receive God's Indescribable Gift: Jesus.

"Sufficient for all your needs" was a warning to keep my eyes from lusting and my mind from fantasizing.

Reflections
The Lord told us about Lust...

"Lust is greed. You can be greedy for anything: sex, food, power, wealth, beauty. When you lust, you set up an altar to worship greed, and you offer your life to satisfy your lust.

"Lust always leads to insanity. Some insane people can pass for normal except in the area where they lack self-control. But eventually their lust corrupts their entire being.

"Lust is the leaven in the meal, and it's never excusable. The demon of lust is that greedy, perverted, jealous, crazy drive in mankind that makes you want what is not yours."

When we were first married, I flirted with other women as I had in my youth. After Barbara called me on it, I attempted to conceal my lust problem rather than conquer it. I ignored the wisdom of Job 31:1-2 (NLT)—

"I made a covenant with my eyes not to look with lust at a young woman."

Lusting is adultery. Jesus said, **"Whoever looks at a woman to lust for her has already committed adultery with her in his heart."**

It was time for me to grow up and put away the immature, hurtful indulgence of lust.

The second storm we weathered was when I was unfaithful with my eyes. I caused a lot of problems and unhappiness in my new family. Fortunately the problem was exposed almost immediately and Barbara confronted me, leaving nowhere to lie or hide. She had compassion on me, came beside me and made it our problem, not my problem.

We spent a lot of time in prayer and I confessed to my pastor and my boss at the ministry where I worked. This was 18 months into our marriage and although we dealt with it, it still took about a year for us to heal.

Barbara: Even though I was hurt, disappointed and appalled, I still cared for Randy's soul. His soul was more important than my pain. I also realized I had been ministering too much and leaving him out. He was less than two years old in his newfound faith. By this time, I had seven years of experience with the Lord and had left some of my own mistakes behind me.

Prior to this, I had to call him on flirting and flattering women. He didn't realize it was a form of unfaithfulness. He was still allowing an ex-girlfriend to call him, and spent hours writing letters to his friend in prison. This was stealing time from us.

Randy stayed up late and watched TV programs I would not approve of. That was evident when the channel would abruptly change when I came downstairs. He learned and repented, and turned loose of those things.

Randy: We became closer and the Lord taught us many valuable lessons.

In a local church in which the pastor was flirtatious but not an outright womanizer, divorces began to occur. First it was the pastor, then it happened to couples in leadership and in the congregation. This was an attack against the whole church. One person said, "We're leaving before that thing jumps on us." People began to leave the church.

In *The Message*, God says in Malachi 2:16, **"I hate the violent dismembering of the 'one flesh' of marriage."** The passage continues, **"So watch yourselves. Don't let your guard down. Don't cheat."**

Chapter 5 – Unfaithfulness

PORNOGRAPHY

We have advised people who confide to us about being trapped in pornography that it is the same as idolatry and adultery. Both are a form of self-pity.

Reflections

The Lord told us about Intimacy...

"The devil wants people (men especially) to substitute selfishness for intimacy in marriage relationships. This drives husband away from wife and wife away from husband, even before debauchery is discovered.

"And who even thinks of it as adultery? If just looking at a woman to lust for her is adultery of the heart, what does that make pornography?

"Adultery is the most treacherous form of idolatry. A man who is unfaithful to his wife is untrustworthy in all things. And an idolater can never experience true intimacy with Me."

PRAY Father, please restore dignity and integrity to men. Help them arise and take their rightful places of leadership in their homes, and in the Body of Christ. Help them be the priests, husbands and parents You intend them to be, walk in their callings, and fulfill their destinies!

In all the power of the Name and Blood of Jesus, set them free from homosexuality, incest and all forms of perversion, and break those powers over families.

Emotional Adultery

Randy: Although Barbara and I have different ways of thinking, we enjoy telling each other everything we experience, think and dream. We share the same philosophy about finances. Since communication and money are the most common problems in a marriage, we know our relationship is greatly blessed.

Still, it took us a long time to see our different personalities as an advantage. In most areas we are so opposite that we used to spend a lot of time trying to fix each other. On our first Christmas, I bought Barbara an expensive suit and boots. She is an artist, and that wasn't her style. There were lots of ways we tried to make each other over.

One day, the Lord intervened and said to us,

> "You two are committing emotional adultery."

We were shocked. We had already moved beyond unfaithfulness in our relationship, and we knew of no other unfaithfulness. The Lord explained,

> "Emotional adultery is when you love the person you want your spouse to be and not the person your spouse is."

No one would ever want to be guilty of any form of adultery in God's eyes. The absence of physical infidelity did not lessen the offense. We knew we were guilty.

"Lord, You're right. But we don't know what to do about it. You must do something in us," Barbara declared.

Because of God's admonishment, we were able to change. I began to tell Barbara I loved her as a whole person, not just selected things about her. This was an expression of commitment. No one feels loved by a spouse with a list of likes and dislikes.

Over time we have learned to love each other because of our differences, not just in spite of them. We thank God that we are not alike, and that we can accomplish much more with the variety of our abilities.

Reflections

The Lord told us about Selfishness...

"How many people do you talk to every week who think they have a problem with their spouse? But ultimately their problem is selfishness.

"To live a full life, you must have gratitude and appreciation. When you encounter people who start to complain about their spouses, you can tell them how helpful it is to make out a list of what they admire, like or love about their spouses. Then they will see they are better people because of their spouses."

"TELL ME YOU LOVE ME"

We've come a long way from when Barbara would say, "Tell me you love me," and I would respond, "When I'm ready." I thought, in order to be sincere, I had to feel it first before I said it. Sometimes that could take awhile. I saw "Tell me you love me" as some sort of test, instead of Barbara's need to be reassured.

Men don't typically experience the kind of insecurities women do. For instance, women are more likely to compare themselves with other women. That was a bad habit the Lord had to break in Barbara. God showed us that whenever we compare ourselves to others, we never come out equal. We either feel inferior and jealous or superior and proud. That is not how He wants us to determine our worth.

Sometimes we compare ourselves to an imaginary standard. That seldom builds our faith or makes us more confident in God. Doing this only made Barbara feel bad about herself. It took her eyes off what God said about her and multiplied her insecurities.

INVESTING TRUST

It was hard for Barbara to trust me. She believed she still had to do everything by herself. Those 9 hard years as a single parent had left an imprint. She learned determination more out of fear than as godly character. If she let up, she believed, she and the children would suffer. That was how they survived. That was the mind-set she brought into our marriage.

I made things worse by being passive at the beginning. The Lord helped us by explaining that trusting is a decision, not an emotion. This applies to trusting God and trusting each other. The Lord told us,

> "Trusting must be done even when the results are in doubt. It's no accomplishment to trust Me when you know how it's going to end."

It took many years for Barbara to learn to trust me. Because of my past, she had good reason not to, and I had to prove myself for a long time. There were times when I felt so judged that I considered going out and doing the things she accused me of because I had nothing to lose. Fear of the Lord prevented me.

This continued until Barbara learned to ask the Lord to teach me in areas she was critical of me. She discovered that works a lot better. I was a lot more open to being taught by God when I wasn't resisting Barbara.

The Lord explained that trust is something we invest. When a spouse or a child feels trusted, they become trustworthy and are more likely to do what is right, He said. And if we invest distrust, they will also respond accordingly. We reap what we sow in others.

"WIVES, ASK YOUR OWN HUSBANDS"

Even though she became a Christian seven years before I did and led me to the Lord, Barbara says she has always looked up to me. But we have known a lot of women who did not respect their husbands. They were critical, disapproving, impatient. Many were divorced in their hearts while still legally married, sharing a name and a house but nothing else. This can be said of men also. Often, the source of their contempt was that their spouses weren't "spiritual."

Early in our marriage, Barbara would ask me for spiritual advice. I felt honored and it made me grow spiritually because I wanted to have the right answers for her. If I didn't know them, I studied to find them, and God gave me wisdom.

Later, Barbara found where I Corinthians 14:35 says, **"And if they (wives) want to learn something, let them ask their own husbands at home"** (NKJV).

We view "ask *your own* husband" as an admonition not to ask other people – like girlfriends or acquaintances or even church leaders. This can unintentionally shame a husband, as if to imply, "My husband isn't spiritual enough to know this."

I once hitched a ride with a man who began to tell me his troubles. "The church stole my wife," he said bitterly. "She was in that place every time the doors were open. I hardly ever saw her when I got home from work. She talked to the preacher about things that were private. It was like she was committing adultery with the church. When I couldn't take it anymore, I left."

When women ask these things of their husbands, the men feel esteemed. This is how wives can build their men up in the faith. It can even bring an unsaved husband to the Lord.

MAKING GOD YOUR SOURCE

Our spouse is not our source for happiness, spirituality or security. God often reminds us about making Him our only source. That concerns a lot more than material provision. He wants us to make Him our source for how we see ourselves.

Whenever we take our eyes off Him, we're like Peter after he stepped out of the boat. As long as he was looking at Jesus, he was fine. But when he surveyed the circumstances around him, he was frightened by the waves and thought he would drown.

The Lord explained to us that when we make anything or anyone our source ahead of Him – possessions, other people, even ourselves – the result is disappointment. He portrayed disappointment as a revolving door which fans in other hindering spirits.

LISTENING TO YOUR HELPER

The Lord told me,

> "If a man doesn't listen to his wife, he won't listen to Me, either."

It seems men are naturally proud. It takes a humble man to listen to his wife. God resists the proud but gives grace to the humble.

It is good for us men to understand that part of honoring our wives is hearing what they have to say, giving them credit for the wisdom they contribute to the household, and loving them with our attitude and not just our words.

Wives often have excellent spiritual discernment – the God-given gift of knowing the origin of a spirit. Wives should be their husbands' preferred confidants and counselors.

Does that mean Barbara always has the right answer? Of course not, and neither do I. It means I recognize that God gave her to me as a helper because I need help.

Husbands can learn a lot from their wives. That is why Proverbs says, **"He who finds a wife finds a good thing, and obtains favor from the Lord"** (18:22 NKJV).

Marriage is the good thing because a wife is not a thing.

In a way I felt relieved when the Lord said, *"If a man doesn't listen to his wife, he won't listen to Me, either."* I wasn't compelled to automatically resist Barbara, and I could safely trust what she told me. It takes time to break old habits and I still have to remind myself about this, but I'm getting better.

Barbara: It took a long time for me to overcome emotional adultery. I was even attacked at night in dreams about Randy doing stupid stuff or not defending me. I repeatedly had to declare, "No, but I love my husband." I am so grateful because now, in our latter years when I have weakness and health issues, he does much of the work I once did, and we are more of a team.

OUR MOST TREASURED TIME

I have always been curious and analytical. The caption under my high school yearbook photo said "Wi Hi's Little Question Box." Randy and I are both communicative. He has a gift of explaining things. So from the very beginning, I asked him everything.

Then one day while praying, we discovered Randy has a gift of hearing the Lord. That changed everything. We spent hours inquiring of the Lord. We got chastised and corrected, but we were also given revelations.

Prayer became our most treasured time with the Lord. We had to discern when we were hearing ourselves and not Him. This was a process. We still ask Him everything.

One day the Lord said to us,

> *"It's hard to hear Me when you have your own opinion."*

We learned to get our opinions and preconceived ideas out on the table before inquiring of the Lord. That way we can hear Him more clearly.

Randy: When Barbara would ask me questions about the Bible, I felt validated and respected. She wasn't trying to trick me, she was just curious. I wanted to find out what it says instead of just give her my opinion. She had a good understanding of the Word, having read the Bible through many times. I wanted to show love to her by taking her requests to heart.

Many times this would lead to a study. I learned how to find the meaning of each word in a passage. This taught me to take my role as spiritual head and priest in my house seriously rather than defer to Barbara because she was more spiritual. It made us both grow in the Lord, and grow closer together.

LISTENING

When we were first married, I was convinced that Barbara didn't listen to me. Truth was, I didn't listen to her either. I was determined to do everything my way, and didn't want a second opinion.

When we discovered God would talk to us, it seemed like everything He said was a correction to me. I had no idea I was doing so many things wrong and had so many impure motives until He pointed them out.

Whenever God brought a correction, it was encased in His love so it didn't sting. The only drawback was, I couldn't keep them to myself. I had to tell Barbara. Even though it hurt my pride to acknowledge them, I had to relate all these reproofs because I did not want to misuse this great gift of hearing Him.

PRAY Father, help me view my spouse as You do, not comparing or complaining. As we are in the process of iron sharpening iron, help me be grateful for my spouse helping me overcome my areas of weakness. Thank You for helping me become more Christlike. Help me look to You and not my spouse to meet all my needs. And help me extend the grace that I want extended to me.

The Orphan Spirit

Randy: I grew up in a functional home, normal by the standards of the '50s and '60s. My parents were attentive and concerned about my well-being. Yet I had a chip on my shoulder. I viewed myself and the world around me through orphan eyes. This hindered my relationships, school achievement and career ambition. It contributed to low expectations and passive behavior.

An orphan spirit rides in on fear and negative emotions to deceive us into feeling unloved, rejected, alone. I was a Christian for 25 years before I recognized this spirit in me. My awareness came through a retired pastor who consented to be a spiritual father to me.

He lived three hours away. Every couple months, we met for lunch. He listened intently as I told him how I was doing. Never judgmental, always encouraging, he would drop questions into the conversation that did not require an answer but always made me think.

He had other sons in his spiritual household. A racially diverse group, we shared his example of love and generosity of spirit.

In the summer of 2009, a half-dozen such households met for a conference. The theme was ruling – not dominating others but learning to control (rule) ourselves by disciplining our emotions and appetites, leading our families in a Christlike fashion, then taking our place of responsibility and authority in the Kingdom of God.

The conference taught how ruling properly is a result of understanding our position of sonship in God's family. If we are duped by an orphan spirit, we cannot rule in a godly manner.

RULING MY HOUSE

Early in our life together, I was admittedly intimidated because Barbara was much more knowledgeable than I about the Bible. When she asked me to lead family devotions, I deferred to her. I let her lead in most spiritual things. I was passive, and Barbara wanted me to be the head. I saw myself as "Mr. Barbara." She wanted to be "Mrs. Walter."

One day she came into my home office and said matter-of-factly, "You're not interceding in the Spirit for me and the children." It wasn't an accusation, just truth. I couldn't dispute it. This prompted me to study what it means to be a family priest and a household head. As I looked in the Scriptures, I Timothy 3:5 (NKJV) got my attention—

"For if a man does not know how to rule his own house, how will he take care of the church of God?"

I studied that verse word by word. Among the meanings attributed to "rule" is "to put ahead of other things." It didn't mean to run with an iron fist or to always have the last word, as I had thought. It meant to serve sacrificially. The household head is to bring his family into the Kingdom of God, and bring God's Kingdom to his family.

After seeming to stall following my salvation experience, my spiritual growth began to accelerate. I realized that God requires a lot of the family head, and also gives him a great allowance of grace and wisdom for the job.

Reflections

The Lord told us about the Orphan Spirit...

"Stop thinking about what you aren't. After all, I'm in charge of what you are and are not. Worrying about what you lack is envy that comes from an orphan spirit.

"Think about what you are. First, be grateful. Second, be content. And third, trust Me that if you need more, I will supply it.

"Gratitude is healing for the orphan spirit."

"I'M AFRAID OF... BECAUSE"

Midway through the fathers and sons conference, we were challenged to write down "I'm afraid of... because." Fear is a hallmark of an orphan, while faith characterizes a son. This exercise was designed to help us recognize and break the influence of the orphan spirit.

I listed my "I'm afraid of" points before writing down my "because" reasons:

- *I'm afraid my personality and conduct won't measure up to God's calling.*
- *I'm afraid doubt will hinder me.*
- *I'm afraid I will not learn to be a good son or father due to fear of relationships.*

- *I'm afraid I won't know how to receive God's provision for my family and ministry.*
- *I'm afraid the way I hear God is tainted by timidity and reluctance to believe Barbara and I can walk out the vision for Shiloh Ministries.*
- *I'm afraid I have sold my* Manna *birthright by failing to speak up when I disagreed, and mindlessly submitting to authority, believing it was all of God.*

I wasn't trying to be spiritual. I wanted to be brutally honest with myself. The things which scare me involve more of the eternal than the temporal. I had seen the pattern of God's faithful provision for so long that I didn't really fear lack. My fear was being like King Belshazzar in the book of Daniel, who was "weighed in the balances and found wanting."

UNMOTIVATED

I was surprised when I started listing the reasons for these fears. The first one was from elementary school.

"Underachiever" is the educator's term for the kind of student I was. I didn't lack the ability to learn, only the motivation. I failed the fourth grade. When I brought home those excruciating report cards, my father always had the same reaction: "If you keep this up, you'll grow up to be a garbage man."

Year after year I heard the same thing. My father was not trying to cast

The Orphan Spirit
1. Operates in fear
2. Anxious about provision and protection
3. Expects failure, rejection, abandonment; preemptively rejects others
4. Insecure about relationships; avoids closeness
5. Has trouble trusting others; leery of those in authority
6. Sacrifices self to please people
7. Feels victimized
8. Critical, judgmental, accusatory, condemning of others and self
9. Interprets disagreement or correction as disapproval and disrespect
10. Feels out of place, unwanted, unappreciated and alone
11. Produces anger
12. Yields to a religious spirit and a spirit of poverty

me into a hopeless future. He was in the military and this was his way of motivating me.

My grades improved by the time I was in high school. I knew I wanted to be a journalist and had started thinking about college. One day my father brought home a *Fortune* magazine which listed, in order of prestige, the top 100 professions in Manhattan. Midway down was one called "sanitation engineer" – garbage man. Six slots below it was "newspaper reporter."

There was some irony in our discovery, but it was also a reminder of my father's reproach. Fifty years later, it was the first thing that came to mind when I considered the reasons for my fears.

The second thing I listed was akin to the first. I didn't sense love from my earthly father. Even though we did things together, we weren't close. There was an awkwardness in our relationship. We never shared the candor and affection which come with love.

The final reason was probably the most revealing. Once when Barbara was receiving a verbal correction from the Lord, she wondered if I deserved one too. Gesturing toward me, she asked God, "What about him?"

It sounded like a passage from the Bible. "Do you love Me?" Jesus asked Peter three times. Stinging from this reproof, Peter saw John, the disciple Jesus loved, and said, "Lord, what about him?"

The Spirit of Adoption

1. Operates in faith
2. Assured that God will meet all needs
3. Feels recognized, successful, desired
4. Secure in relationships; comfortable being known
5. Trusts others; respects authority; willing to submit
6. Able to give up personal rights without being resentful
7. Confident as an overcomer
8. Compassionate and patient with others; able to see past their flaws
9. Receives constructive criticism without taking it personally
10. Feels included, comfortable, unselfconscious in most environments
11. Produces peace
12. Certain of God's love and acceptance

When Barbara asked that question, the Lord's answer to us was, "I don't have much trouble with him." That should have sounded like I didn't need a rebuke, but I heard it with orphan ears. To me it said, **"I don't want to take much time with him."**

I was interpreting my relationship with my Heavenly Father through the disappointments in my relationship with my earthly father.

GOD'S RESPONSE

There it was, all out in the open. I was no longer stuffing my fears and trying to hide from them. Rather than ask prayer from the members of my spiritual household, I sensed God Himself was going to minister to me.

I listened for His responses to the reasons for my fears. He made me chuckle when He said about the "garbage man" stigma—

"That's obviously not your destiny. Let go of it."

I had carried that baggage for way too long. It was time to get over my offense. One revelation from God and I was totally free. I needed to learn to love Him more, so I could love others the way He loves me. Then He said,

> "Your father's inability to express himself means you don't know what he felt. You were his pride. He looked to you to excel his accomplishments. He wanted better for you than he saw in himself. I have brought his desires to pass.
>
> "Don't stay stuck in judgment which perpetuates old wounds. See the freedom you have and be eager to walk in greater liberty.
>
> "Don't replace Me with your father's image – that is idolatry. Worship Me for who I AM. Don't imagine rejection if you truly seek Me. I AM not contrary. When I say you will find Me when you seek Me with your whole heart, it is an invitation, not a threat."

Barbara: I grew up in a pretty functional home also. But maybe because we moved so much, as far back as I could remember, I knew the pain of feeling like I didn't belong, even in my own family.

I was the second of four girls. I often asked myself, "What's wrong with me?" I only felt loved by my older sister. I don't remember any other friend until the third grade. I attended many different schools because our family moved around. Repeating the second grade made me feel stupid and rejected. I recall being isolated and sad. At one school, my only playmates were the acorns that fell from a tree in the schoolyard.

I didn't know at the time that I was feeling rejection. A spirit of rejection causes you to easily take and readily give offense. It makes you critical and judgmental. It provokes you to reject others before they can do it to you. It makes you feel bad about yourself. That's how the cycle of being rejected continues. The spirit of rejection is part of the orphan spirit. This was so deep-seated in me that I was in my 50s when the Lord finally delivered me from it.

> "I AM the Father of all fathers, and I don't require you to speak My language, so I speak yours."

Reflections

The Lord told us about Rejection...

"You can come to the place where knowing, serving and glorifying Me is enough. That is where the power is. The power is not in defending yourself against undeserved rejection. Jesus never did that.

"When Jesus walked the earth, He was constantly in the shadow of the cross. Even the black foreboding of unimaginable suffering could not make Him defend Himself. Everything He did – which was everything righteous – drew Him nearer to the cross.

"He saw seasons of favor with men and experienced the ultimate rejection of men. He received both adulation and mocking. In the same week, the people wanted to make Him their king, and then others crowned Him with thorns.

"His strength was to do My will. It was His passion and His very life. No man could kill Him without His consent. He died willingly. Why? Because of the joy of obeying His Father and the hope of redeeming mankind. For that purpose, He came to Earth.

"What should you learn from this? Obedience to Me provides the joy which produces strength, even in the face of pain, whether it is from physical injury or emotional hurt."

Reflections

The Lord told us about Condemnation...

"Your worst feeling is not being loved. When you blame yourself (which is different than taking responsibility and confessing sin), you are not loving yourself. You are not loving the gift I made you to be. You are not grateful for your existence. And when you don't love yourself, you don't feel loved.

"That's why the enemy continuously tries to feed you with condemnation — to make you despise who you are and what you've done. He knows that if you cannot receive My love, you will believe and do anything. If you do receive My love, you will have self-discipline and obey My statutes that are for your own good.

"If you know Me and sense My love, you won't listen to the condemnation of the enemy; you will accept the gift of My grace and be grateful for the process of redeeming you from all the things the enemy accuses you of."

PRAY  Father, help me find my identity in You, not in my lineage, culture, or social status. Help me believe what You say about me, that I am greatly blessed, highly favored and deeply loved — that I am so loved and accepted that You sent Jesus to die for me so I could be in Your family. I declare that I am valuable, unique, and have a purpose in Your Kingdom because You say so.

Atmosphere for Increase

Randy: As Barbara and I were praying, the Lord taught us a life-changing principle which triumphs over the orphan spirit. We repeat it to one another on an almost daily basis: "Gratitude creates an atmosphere for increase."

It reminds us that every blessing comes from God. What have we gotten through our own merit, even by hard labor, that God hasn't given to us?

When God told us this principle, Barbara and I were asking Him why some other couples we know, who earn three or four times our income, seem to live hand-to-mouth while we prosper on so much less. We were reminded, "Gratitude creates an atmosphere for increase."

He was saying that gratitude prospers us more than wealth. Prosperity is not only financial, it is spiritual.

An orphan heart fears lack and is seldom content. It is the ultimate embezzler because it steals the capacity to be grateful. The Lord told us,

> "Fear is often anxiety over lack. If you believe I supply all your needs, then you have no fear. Any area where you're tempted to be anxious is where the deceiver has convinced you that you will suffer lack because I will not provide."

A SPIRIT OF POVERTY

A few months after receiving the revelation "Gratitude creates an atmosphere for increase," I was listening to a secular radio interview. The principle of gratitude and increase was confirmed when the guest stated its corollary: **"Ingratitude invites a spirit of poverty."**

What an eye-opening statement. It reveals the enemy's method of keeping people from receiving all God has for them so they feel neglected, mistreated, poor and sorry for themselves. When a man feels sorry for himself, no one else will, and few people want to help him. The spirit of poverty becomes a self-fulfilling prophecy.

Barbara and I often tell each other how rich we feel. This doesn't come from a savings account or stock portfolio because we don't have those things. Our investments have been in eternal things, and we know our rewards will follow suit. We are guided by Jesus' words in Matthew 6:19, 33 (NLT)—

"Don't store up treasures here on earth, where moths eat them and rust destroys them, and where thieves break in and steal. Store your treasures in heaven, where moths and rust cannot destroy, and thieves do not break in and steal.... Seek the Kingdom of God above all else, and live righteously, and He will give you everything you need."

Reflections
The Lord told us about Gratitude...

"A poverty spirit will keep you focused on yourself.

"Gratitude produces favor, and favor multiplies blessings.

"The attitude of gratitude, combined with trusting Me, is the fulfillment of 'Seek first the Kingdom of God and His righteousness and He will meet all your needs.'

"Gratitude is a key for moving on in your life. Wherever you feel stuck, it's because you're not grateful.

"Every morning, think of your family members – one at a time – beginning with your spouse. Acknowledge what I have done in their lives and thank Me out loud. Let this mind of gratitude also be in you which was in Christ Jesus.

"Even though they're closely related, poverty and jealousy are distinctly different. Entitlement links them together. When entitlement does not want to be detected, it produces shame."

BEING GOOD STEWARDS

Barbara: The Lord is continuing to teach us how to be good stewards – wise managers of what He provides. He told us to pray for our stewardship skills as He releases more to us. I pray daily for Him to show us ways to reduce our bills and live in His abundant economy.

Reflections

The Lord told us about Wisdom and Money...

"A lot of people want material things from Me. Very few people ask Me for wisdom. When people ask Me for wisdom, they are seeking first My Kingdom, and all their needs are provided.

"I don't want money to be anybody's source. And I don't want money to be anybody's savior.

"Money is the world system. While you're in the world, you have to do some things the world's way. The problem with money is when people venerate it. That's when it becomes a god and they seek it ahead of Me.

"Learning how to operate by Kingdom methods takes your solutions beyond money, so money is not the only answer. That's when it becomes a means of exchange but not the love of a man's heart. Then money can be seen as a tool and not life's ultimate objective. My Word says very deliberately, 'The love of money is a root of all evil.'

"Money can't provide security. Notice that the more of it people have, the less secure they often are. Fear of loss is greater than fear of lack. That's why money is a trap. That is the deceitfulness of riches.

"I AM disciplining you to see money as a tool and not a goal. This is the root belief of generosity – when money is not owned but used. I've told you before that money by itself is not valuable. It actually is a means of agreement for making trades.

"Money is as much for training as for paying. I bring small amounts of money to you to see how faithfully you will handle it. When you steward well the little things, I increase you to bigger ones.

"I AM teaching you not only about money's value for purchasing things. I AM teaching you how to esteem it as one, but not the only resource for getting things done. I want you to see yourself as needing more than money. This is a breaking process where I chip the world away from you so your thinking will be Kingdom and not carnal."

We both agree on our budget and tithing. Even though Randy takes care of the finances because he is gifted in that area, we do nothing without agreement. Because our income is only enough to cover our basic bills, we pray together for God to supply the extra resources for food, property taxes, repairs and other additional expenses. Although we still worry at times, He has been totally faithful.

We often remind ourselves of the account of the Hebrew children in the wilderness gathering manna. Those who gathered too much had nothing leftover, and those who didn't gather enough had plenty.

When we were first married, I had my own checking account. But as all my money was needed for bills, we closed it because it cost to keep it open. Now when I have a special need or want, I just ask the Lord and He blesses me or changes my mind about it.

Reflections

The Lord told us about Finances and Ministry...

"How many people have the heart and the gifts to minister effectively, but are out of position because their finances are a mess? They must spend so much time patching their financial inner tube that they are too distracted to work for the Kingdom.

"Everything is directed at the harvest. The whole Kingdom is directed at the harvest. But right now, your purpose is not to announce the harvest; it's to position people to use their gifts for the Kingdom."

"BE ANXIOUS FOR NOTHING"

Randy: In the middle of a muggy 100-degree heat wave, just before a visit from Barbara's sister, our central air conditioning quit. Barbara and I immediately agreed not to worry about repair expenses but be grateful, even with company on the way.

It took two sweltering days to get in touch with our HVAC guy, but we maintained an attitude of gratitude, looking to God as our source. The problem turned out to be a part that was under warranty so there was no charge. The repair was completed in the nick of time. But that wasn't all we had to be grateful for.

Our HVAC guy has been a wonderful friend. He offered to pull some strings and get us complimentary tickets for an expensive dinner cruise on the Potomac River in Washington, D.C. – something we could not afford on our own. We asked if we could take another couple along and he made the arrangements.

We invited friends who pastor a church to go with us so we could celebrate the wife's 50th birthday. We didn't know until that evening that she had asked the Lord for a special gift – to go on a cruise.

One of my life verses is Philippians 4:6-7 (NKJV) —

"Be anxious for nothing, but in everything by prayer and supplication, with thanksgiving, let your requests be made known to God; and the peace of God, which surpasses all understanding, will guard your hearts and minds through Christ Jesus."

Because we didn't panic and kept thanking God for our circumstances, He blessed us and we were able to bless our friends. The tickets would have cost $300, but we went as special guests.

Gratitude created an atmosphere for increase.

Reflections

The Lord told us about Arguing over Money...

"Nothing brings out more selfishness, more carnality and more unabated anger than when people argue over money.

"Even marital infidelity sometimes is not as provocative as when couples fight over finances.

"The sociologists say differences over money cause marriages to disintegrate. I say differences over money are symptoms of selfishness which is already causing the marriage to disintegrate."

DISAGREEMENT OVER FINANCES

Barbara: The Lord told us this principle: "How can you get what you already have?" It sounded like a puzzle, but a few days later He demonstrated this principle to us. We had gone to a 6 a.m. prayer meeting in a nearby town. After we ate breakfast, most stores were still not open.

I needed to get a toilet seat and a plastic table cloth. I didn't want to spend more than a dollar for the table cloth, and I had previously bought four new toilet seats on sale for two dollars each, but they were already installed. So I was looking for another great deal.

After we looked in two building supply stores, Randy broke out laughing when he remembered we still had a new toilet seat in the shed. Just after that, the Lord reminded me that I also had a new plastic table cloth in the laundry room. It was a clear instance of *"How can you get what you already have?"*

We try to keep this in mind when we are looking to purchase items, because we might already have them. Sometimes the Lord shows us we don't even need what we thought we did. He helps us be frugal.

Jesus instructed us to pray that we be good stewards over what we already have and, at the same time, learn to live in His abundance. Because we have been faithful and good stewards, He has made us responsible over more.

Randy: To me, *"How can you get what you already have?"* is God's way of reminding us that we already possess all things. Romans 8:32 (NKJV) says, **"He who did not spare His own Son, but delivered Him up for us all, how shall He not with Him also freely give us all things?"**

As His children, He promises to supply our needs by His riches. We needn't worry or beg, but trust Him for what He has already promised.

How can we receive again what we've already been given?

Reflections
The Lord told us about Vanity...

"What keeps men from recognizing and acknowledging Me? Vanity, riches and deception. Before you think of vanity as looking in the mirror, consider what Solomon said about it – that the pursuit of life apart from Me is vanity.

"Man's strength and accomplishments are vanity. All pursuits aside from Me are vanity, which frustrates the spirit. Vanity is selfishness. Pursuing Me is godliness. Every man chases what is at the center of his life.

"Say 'riches' to a man who thinks he is poor and he will scoff at you. But riches depend on your standard of comparison. To a man convinced of his poverty, what he has is never enough. That's what keeps him ungrateful and prevents him from prospering.

"Remember that gratitude is stewardship of your future."

Chapter 8 – Atmosphere for Increase

Reflections

The Lord told us about Striving...

"I assigned Adam to till the ground. He had to work to produce food, but he knew I was the source. Men have to learn how to be productive without becoming their own source.

"When you strive, that does not mean just exerting yourself. It means trying to take My place because you've become your own source. Striving is what Lucifer did.

"It's a law of the universe that whatever you do brings some kind of return. If you do nothing, your return is lack. If you invest wisely, your return is profit. If you exercise faith, your return is authority. Any gesture you make yields a return.

"The first indicator of striving is lack of contentment. That will push a man to contend for what his hands can grasp. If you are striving for riches or recognition or other earthly gain, you are contending with Me to see who will be its source. Striving is self-defeating, even if it doesn't look like it at first, because it is pride which I resist."

PRAY Father, You have taught us to be good stewards, diligent, and frugal. So please help me trust You with our finances and stop worrying. Help me not have entitlement or foolish thinking. And show me when I am rebelling against common sense.

Reveal to me any area where I have failed to give or tithe properly, or tried to manipulate You with my giving. Help me rightly divide Your Word on finances. Teach me to prosper Your way.

Help me live in Your abundant economy and be a cheerful, generous giver. Cause Your favor to rest on me, and establish the work of my hands.

Where Do You Hurt/Hide?

Randy: People can be married for many years and still hide from each other.

Barbara and I are sometimes approached by people seeking advice. The Lord told us not to ask what they have or have not done, but to ask, "Where do you hurt? Where do you hide?" We began to think about what that means for us.

WHY DO WE HIDE?

Hiding: What causes it? What are its negative ramifications? How do we recognize it? How do we come out of it? We hide because we hurt.

"Hide from what? I'm not hiding," most of us think. Suppose "hiding" were defined as failing to place our whole confidence in God? It would be the condition of fallen man.

The first incidence of hiding was in the Garden of Eden. Adam and Eve hid themselves from God.

"Then the Lord God called to Adam and said to him, 'Where are you?' So he said, 'I heard Your voice in the garden, and I was afraid because I was naked; and I hid myself'" (Genesis 3:9-10 NKJV).

It wasn't only an awareness that Adam and Eve were without clothing, which they had never worn. They perceived that the mantle of God's glory which had covered them was gone. Now their flesh had to provide its own protection. They recognized nakedness as vulnerability, became afraid, and hid. Men have been trying to hide from God ever since.

With the knowledge of good and evil came the realization that Adam and Eve surrendered their authority and forfeited the intimacy they had known with God. They exchanged life for death. Imagine the agony and shame of their new reality! When they hid from God, they were also trying to hide from their pain. They hid because they hurt.

After the Fall, they and their descendants lived in a world which soon became like the one we know today. Corruption, violence and hiding from God increased rapidly. Hiding feeds shame, fear and an orphan mind-set.

ORPHANS?

How could men, who were created in God's image to have a relationship with Him, end up feeling like orphans? My wife, Barbara, and I asked the Lord that question, and He replied,

> "It came in when man developed a sense of himself separate from Me. Sin divided us and gave him a different identity. At the beginning, we were one. After the Fall, man started recreating himself, and he opened the door to thinking like an orphan.
>
> "Ever since, man has tried to develop his own identity. The more focused he is on himself, the less open and aware he was of Me. In the beginning, we processed everything together. Now he tries to placate Me rather than receive Me. He still hides in an attempt to conceal his sin."

Sin separates us from God, and makes us believe we can hide ourselves and what we do from Him.

"'Can anyone hide himself in secret places, so I shall not see him?' says the Lord; 'Do I not fill heaven and earth?' says the Lord" (Jeremiah 23:24 NKJV).

Yet men attempt to conceal themselves from God anyway. It is futile to hide from God physically, but we can still try to do it emotionally.

Just as hiding doesn't work in our relationship with God, it doesn't work in a marriage either.

FEAR OF BEING KNOWN

One couple who requested our help had no stability, frequently moving from place to place and job to job. Even as they struggled financially, they strove to be recognized as ministry leaders. When we prayed about what to say to them, the Lord called this "being flighty" due to "fear of being known."

Hiding is an attempt to obscure something. The opposite is to reveal or confess. One of the meanings of "occult" is to be hidden, referring to secret knowledge and practices.

Hiding is not just when you place yourself off limits to others. It can be done by finding your identity in an inappropriate place.

Do you know someone who identifies so strongly with a cause or another person that it becomes the reason for his existence? He is hiding his real self behind something or someone else. Name-dropping is one way to do this – mentioning well-known people to impress others, inferring that a relationship exists where it does not. We hide because we are ashamed.

Reflections

The Lord told us about Shame...

"At first, recognition is fulfilling. But soon after that need is met, recognition can lead to fear. Rejection seems to hide behind every form of intimacy. Running is a way to avoid it.

"All this is rooted in shame, and shame is one of the most unteachable spirits. It agrees but does not learn, due to fear of exposure. Its style is to endear but never to commit, and its fruit is the very thing the person is trying to avoid – rejection.

"Shame uses dishonesty until that person no longer knows what is real. It blames and hides when the things it wants are out of reach. The longview of being flighty is desolation and self-destruction.

"Fear of being known is the biggest insecurity of all. It means you don't think you can trust anyone, so you hold everybody at bay, and then you feel lonely. Worst of all, not being able to trust anyone includes Me."

HIDING BEHIND RELIGION

It is also possible to hide behind a religious belief system. That is how Jesus regarded the scribes and Pharisees. He told the people to obey what they said but not to be like them because **"they say, and do not do"** (Matthew 23:3 NKJV). The scribes and Pharisees used their authority for personal gain. To ensure their positions, they mercilessly subjugated the people to the rigor of the Law.

The thought that I might be hiding behind a spiritual façade never occurred to me until one morning in church. I had been in a conspicuous public ministry for 20 years. It was a demanding position. I thought I was giving God my best. So it came as a shock when, sitting smugly in a worship service, I heard a quiet voice whisper in my spirit, *"You're hiding in here."*

I had been more concerned with appearance and approval from men than with total obedience. I was doing part of what God assigned to me, but hiding from other things He told me to do. I wasn't much different from Jonah, except I was trying to hide in God's house behind a pretense of works.

I could see that I was like the scribes and Pharisees who loved greetings in the marketplace, the best places at feasts and the best seats in the synagogues. Jesus said what they did was to be seen by men, and called them "hypocrites." They could not hide their greed and indifference from Him.

I also hid from Barbara. We think we're hiding from what has or might hurt us, so we don't see it as backsliding. But when we're hiding, we are not giving our best. If our relationship with God is a mirror image of our relationship with our spouse, we are not giving Him our best either.

People typically don't think of hiding as avoiding our spiritual calling or neglecting God's assignment for us. We've heard some say, "I'm just waiting for God to show me what my ministry is." Meanwhile, they're doing nothing of eternal consequence. In fact, they are hiding from His will and blaming Him for the delay. If God hasn't given them a specific assignment, the Bible is full of ministry instructions that everyone is called to follow.

We can also hide from other people, including our families. We don't want them to see the things that embarrass us – our failures, fears, character flaws and inadequacies. Bluff and bluster replace honesty and accountability. We become self-conscious rather than God-confident. Fear of man, including a spouse, makes any situation all about us instead of what God can do through us.

Reflections

The Lord told us about Putting our Light under a Basket...

"Hiding by keeping your fine qualities to yourself is an escalated form of selfishness. That is the deeper meaning of putting your light under a basket – much more than just failing to be evangelical.

"I made every person with the potential to be a gift to those around them. By not being generous with yourself out of fear, you undermine My purpose for your existence. This is the pitfall of fearing the rejection of man. Fear causes everyone to suffer loss."

HIDING FROM GOD

"If you hide from God, wisdom will hide from you."

When we hide from God, we are hiding from His goodness. Romans 2:4 says the goodness of God brings a man to repentance. We are to be containers of His character and conductors of His power. When we hide from Him, we can actually keep others from being saved.

Many of us know people who appear to have good hearts, yet they live in defiance of God's commands. Despite the goodness they seem to possess, they are closed to Him. Even if they are willing to talk about the Lord, there is no desire to learn about or obey Him. It's very sad to watch them pay the price for their rebellion, and to realize they may not change. How easy it is to label them "lost" without asking ourselves where they hurt and what makes them hide.

Hiding from God is like erecting a NO TRESPASSING sign to protect the parts of us that we refuse to surrender. We don't want Him or others to see them – as if we could outwit the One who **"searches all hearts and understands all the intent of the thoughts"** (I Chronicles 28:9 NKJV).

He knows us better than we know ourselves; He still loves us with an everlasting love; and His purpose is to do us good and not harm. Rather than posting portions of ourselves OFF LIMITS to God and others, our challenge is learning to trust Him with every aspect of who we are.

DOING THINGS OUR WAY

How often do we do things alone without asking for God's help? Even if we aren't doing anything wrong and have nothing to conceal from Him, excluding God from our activities is really a demonstration of pride.

If we're undertaking something by ourselves, even if out of obedience, it is still secretive, as though done in darkness rather than in His sight. We forget that in our weakness (inability, sickness, human limitations), He wants to demonstrate His strength. Refusing to allow His power to be revealed through us is like trying to hide our imperfections, ignorance and helplessness. Whenever we take credit for our gifts and achievements, we not only hide from Him but hide Him from others.

Are we depending on God? Do we want to give Him credit or take it ourselves? Perhaps that is why, once when I asked Him to take care of a concern, He responded, *"The problem isn't the problem. The problem is you."*

We also try to hide by ignoring the need to revere God, as in Malachi 1:6, where God upbraided the people for expecting Him not to notice when they offered sick and blemished sacrifices. **"Where is My reverence?"** He said.

WHERE DO WE HIDE?

Hiding is demonic. Demons try to hide where and what they are.

Men try to hide from God in the world that accommodates their fears. It's the only place dark enough that they think He won't see them. The apostle John wrote that men **"loved darkness instead of light because their deeds were evil. Everyone who does evil hates the light, and will not come into the light for fear that their deeds will be exposed"** (John 3:19-20 NIV).

Pornography fits this description. Many times when wives expose their husband's sin or faults, they are resented for it. In reality, the wife is usually just trying to help her husband, and has his best interest at heart.

Chapter 9 – Where Do You Hurt/Hide?

Sometimes this is reversed, but generally speaking it's the men who need correcting, especially when it comes to pornography.

Like chameleons, men act as the world acts to try to conceal themselves. And the world accepts its own by telling them it's okay to ignore God. Repentance is the only thing that changes the way we act. It is not just telling God we're sorry and asking His forgiveness – it is a shift in how we think, which transforms how we behave.

Before I repented and was spiritually reborn, I hid in the world. I identified with bad people. To fit in, I tried to be like them, secretly believing I was superior so I could feel good about myself. I hid because, deep inside, I feared failure and I feared success. Failure generated rejection, and success might require more than I wanted to give.

Now I see hiding for what it is – *SELFISHNESS*. I recognize the things I have hidden behind. When I feel insecure, I'm still tempted to use these things as a smokescreen so people won't see me, even Barbara.

Here is a partial list of things I have hidden behind, and the way the Lord explained them to me. Can you relate to any of them?

- **INTELLECTUALISM/RELIGION** – for the sake of impressing others, talking without being committed to what I advocate.
- **ABILITIES/GIFTEDNESS** – finding identity in what I do rather than who God says I am.
- **SELF-PITY** – entitlement pandering for sympathy.
- **UNFORGIVENESS** – unwillingness to release the past.
- **PROCRASTINATION/PERFECTIONISM** – waiting until conditions are perfect, which never happens, before moving ahead.
- **MAN-PLEASING** – changing who I am to meet the expectations of others so I can manipulate them.
- **CHURCH** – putting in an appearance to be seen by men.
- **MINISTRY** – using position as a front with which to impress rather than a platform from which to serve.
- **DUTY** – obedience without passion becomes joyless, and reduces a relationship with God to little more than a philosophical belief system.
- **PERSONAL APPEARANCE** – relying on how I look (good or bad), so people won't know the real me.
- **ENTERTAINMENT** – gratifying myself rather than pleasing God.
- **RESISTING/STUBBORNNESS** – opposite of being humble, teachable.

STUBBORNNESS

When God teaches us, He doesn't want to merely add to our knowledge; He wants to change our hearts. I have intellectualized many things I should have internalized. Without realizing it, I tried to use that knowledge to influence others rather than become more Christlike. That is another form of hiding.

It scared me when I read in I Samuel 15:23 (NKJV), **"For rebellion is as the sin of witchcraft, and stubbornness is as iniquity and idolatry."** I recognized stubbornness in myself as a passive attempt at manipulation. That scripture equates stubbornness to idol worship and witchcraft.

Witchcraft does not have to be performed by witches. Usually, it is when a person with unforgiveness is trying to manipulate others.

Reflections

The Lord told us about Witchcraft...

"Witchcraft is not just spells and potions. My Word says it is rebellion, and rebellion is always against authority. So when trying to identify where witchcraft comes against you, don't just consider nameless, faceless people who oppose your beliefs. Look at the people under your authority. Even if they are not consciously trying to undermine you, if they are using techniques of rebellion and disobedience and disrespect, it accomplishes witchcraft."

DUTY

What a loaded word "duty" is. On the surface it suggests responsibility and faithfulness – visible qualities of obedience. Duty in itself is not a bad thing. How can it be a place to hide?

Duty does not require passion. We lose the vitality of a relationship with the Lord and with others if devotion degenerates into duty. When obedience is mechanical and life is all about ourselves, then duty becomes a place to hide rather than grow. Duty can rob us of our zeal. We no longer love with abandon, live with joy, and trust without reservation. Even worship can become a duty rather than a response to the Lord. Our marriages suffer when we perform duty without cherishing.

Barbara needed lots of physical assistance due to a very painful back condition. When she said one day that I was helping her out of a sense of duty rather than love, I had to confess she was right. I was putting duty ahead of my devotion to Barbara, and she saw right through it, which made her feel worse. She felt unloved, like a burden, and not cherished. This was not conducive to her healing but, in fact, it perpetuated her pain. I asked her forgiveness, changed my thinking, and she said my actions showed it.

Joyless obedience causes the world to view our faith as little more than a belief system, not a vibrant bond with the Creator of the universe. Duty can reduce Christianity to toeing the line and striving to get to heaven. Duty without devotion is, at best, self-satisfying and not an expression of love.

When duty is subject to a man-pleasing spirit, it says, "As long as I'm doing what's right, you won't see the real me and you can't criticize me," or, "I am a good servant, so you don't have the right to require anything else."

The Lord told me,

> "Son, you hide behind being responsible (dutiful). While this is commendable because it is for My Kingdom, it becomes an idol if you put it ahead of Me."

Reflections

The Lord told us about Being Misunderstood...

"Fear of being misunderstood, disregarded or embarrassed has to do with image. What if Jesus had those fears while He was on Earth? It would have cluttered the way to His destiny. When He made Himself of no reputation, He gave up the right to those fears.

"Jesus did not insist on being understood or acknowledged. He was the King of Glory, without palace or possessions. He had more power than anyone could imagine, but did not use it to make Himself look good. That's being unselfconscious.

"This is part of the burden of your cross. If you complain while you're carrying your cross, are you truly following Jesus?

"Being misunderstood is the hardest offense to get over because it makes you feel the most helpless. Wasn't Jesus misunderstood? And yet He chose not to take offense. Why? Because of love.

"Duty and proving yourself don't know that kind of love. Working hard and achieving results don't develop that kind of love, even when you labor to help other people. Such love is an attitude of the heart, not an achievement of the hands. It overlooks offense, which is the real meaning of 'Love covers a multitude of sins.'"

BEING MISUNDERSTOOD

Hiding insulates us from relationships. It is pain management, a form of self-medication. One of the most convenient places to hide is in feeling misunderstood. Our intentions are called into question; and usually, no amount of explanation can rectify the situation. This leads to more fear and hiding. People also do this in marriage.

Reflections

The Lord told us about Unforgiveness and Shame...

"Unforgiveness sours your future and makes it hard to receive love. Unforgiveness in one relationship makes it hard to forgive in other relationships. Forgiveness is necessary in all relationships. The better you get at it, the more friends you will have, the better friend you will be, and the more like Me you will become.

"Feeling unloved causes shame. You deduce that something is wrong with you. If you don't know where your shame comes from, it's harder to release. Shame is not natural and it's not permanent. It's a deception that says nothing is powerful enough to remove it.

"Shame replicates itself. Shame comes because of sin, and alters your behavior to produce more sin. The only way out is believing in the sacrifice of Jesus, repenting, and allowing Me to set you free.

"Being covered with shame is the extreme. It is a shroud of death. When it's guilt over a lifetime, not one single event, it becomes how you see yourself. You need to line up with how I see you. Then you can forsake what the enemy wants you to think.

"Someone with shame will be ingratiating, not to honor the other person but to subordinate himself to the lower level he thinks he deserves. People will see his self-hatred and treat him shamefully. In turn, he will act shamefully and blame it on them.

"What is the opposite of feeling bad about yourself? Feeling good about yourself. When you only feel good about the things you've done, it doesn't last long and it becomes an addiction.

"Feeling good about who you are draws you into My destiny for your life. It incorporates sonship and your distinct nature into a concept of how uniquely valuable you are. This is not conceit but alignment with your creation purpose. It breaks off shame."

UNFORGIVENESS

Barbara: We have two women friends who were married to narcissists. Both husbands are now dead. Although these men looked good to others, their wives received the brunt of their cruelty at home. Both of these husbands had suffered abuse as children, and had deep-seated unforgiveness in their hearts which transferred to emotional abuse of their wives.

Unforgiveness needs to be dealt with as soon as possible, before it consumes a person.

PRAY Father, help me be honest with You, myself and my spouse. Forgive me for trying to hide the real me from You and others. Please bring to the light every dark area of shame, guilt and pride that keeps me from wanting Your light and truth. Set me free. Show me areas where I still have unforgiveness, resentment and fear, and deliver me.

Make me an example of godliness that my spouse cannot resist. Comfort me and help me keep my eyes on You. Increase my faith and replace my hurt with joy.

Disciplining our Emotions

Barbara: Randy and I had little understanding of discipline in our emotions. My parents were good people with good reputations, but I never had a significant conversation with my father. I didn't feel like his little girl, just one of his four daughters. I was never spanked or disciplined except occasionally being yelled at by my mother.

Randy and I carried our childhood wounds into our marriage. Although he and I had many deep and meaningful conversations, he was passive like my father. That hurt my feelings and I learned not to trust him. Randy thought that if he clammed up, whatever issue I was having would go away. In reality, it just got worse. It made me mad, and even madder when he would smile and pretend that everything was okay. I saw it as wimping out, and I felt unloved.

Reflections

The Lord told us about Fear...

"What makes you afraid to receive My comfort? Fear that if you don't take charge, nothing will get done? Fear that it's all up to you? Fear that you're not able? Fear that there isn't enough and that all your efforts won't be enough? Fear that in spite of My words, I don't love you?

"All these fears concern protection and provision. Compared to everything else, see how these fears carry so much more weight?

"You both have to learn to discipline your emotions, just like when you learned to regulate your extremes so the highs won't be too high and your lows aren't too low" (reference to being bipolar).

Reflections

The Lord told us about Siding with the Accuser...

"If you make Randy your source, you're going to be angry, sick and disappointed for the rest of your life. Moreover, you will find yourself siding with the accuser.

"If you want to live well and not be sick, you need to learn self-control in this area. If you weren't married to Randy, do you think you could find a man who would live up to all your requirements? What you are really looking for is a wimp who won't be wimpy. There are none.

"You have to agree to respect each other; then everything else will fall into line. So be patient and turn off the 'Automatic Annoyance' setting – both of you. When there is something in you that works against each other, it's a waste of energy. And it's not just one of you.

"Stop finding fault and stop feeling overly sensitive about being contradicted. Lay down your rights, take up the desire to minister to each other, and you will get everything done and have fun."

CONTROL-RESIST

The Lord began to parent both of us all over again. We were so immature and we both tried to fix our unhappy situation with the only mechanism we knew – controlling. The Lord taught us that when one tries to control, the other resists.

All the while God was teaching us, He was still using us in ministry, flaws and all. He doesn't wait until we are all better, He teaches us as we go. He made us feel loved and valued.

As my children were growing up, I treated them the same way I was treated, trying to gain control by yelling. But I added the missing ingredient – punishment by spanking. Except I did it in anger, harming their souls.

God had a new reality for Randy and me. He gave me this to read daily:

• I perceive that reality is not what my senses detect; reality is the unshakable truth of God's Word.

• I declare that as my faith is tested, I will grow into the measure of God's joy for me.

Randy: In traffic, I would get angry at other drivers. Even though they couldn't hear what I was saying, they could see my mouth moving. The Lord broke me of this habit when someone pulled out in front of me onto a highway. With the cruise control set on 55, I had to lock up the brakes. When a collision appeared unavoidable, it seemed like a large invisible hand swerved my car away from the other one. We missed by a couple inches.

Obviously shaken, the other driver pulled over. I smiled a big smile and waved as if to say, "I'm glad you're all right," and drove away. After that, the anger was gone. Now when someone irritates me, I don't use the same language. Sometimes I still make a derogatory comment and Barbara reminds me, "It's not all about you. Why are you cursing yourself?" I've learned that anything negative I say about the other person can come back on me.

PEACE VS. OFFENSE

These are some of the areas in which we have to discipline our emotions:

**COMPETITION • BLAMING • ANGER • FEAR
RESENTMENT (THE FRUIT OF SELF-PITY)
DISCOURAGEMENT • UNFORGIVENESS • ENABLING**

Reflections
The Lord told us about Blaming...

"When there is no peace, there is always blaming. Do you believe you can have peace no matter what anyone says or does to you?

"If it is no longer you who live but I live in you, then it is no longer you who are insulted, and there is no reason for you to take offense. It's only when you defend yourself that people become your enemies, and living deteriorates to survival.

"Peace and favor go hand in hand. Being a carrier of peace shows favor to those around you; and as you do to them, it is done to you.

"You can see how blaming spoils everything. It makes life a struggle. That's why it was so important that I gave My followers My peace, which overcame every obstacle to My obedience.

"You know you are commissioned to take the Gospel and make disciples. How effective can you be without peace? In the world, you are just one more voice clamoring to be right if you lack peace. But when you possess true peace, people will want to hear what you have to say."

Chapter 10 – Disciplining our Emotions

STRESS

The Lord showed us that undisciplined emotions result in stress. Stress does not come with our circumstances; stress is our response to them. We may not have control over what happens, but by disciplining our emotions, we can determine whether stress gets the better of us.

Stress is the source of sickness. Undisciplined emotions and lies produce gods in our lives. Barbara and I didn't realize we had gods in our lives. The Lord showed me that my god was, "Unless I do it myself, it won't get done right. No one else knows how to do it but me, so I need to do everything." What a setup for perfectionism and procrastination!

Self-pity and resentment are my greatest weaknesses. The Lord added,

> "Self-pity does not give you a license to be contrary or take out your frustrations on other people. Until you take equal blame and responsibility, life just becomes a contest of accusations.
>
> "Many people believe that avoiding a confrontation is humility while they complain bitterly in their souls. What a miserable way to live.
>
> "Resentment results when you don't feel like you can talk freely. It makes you feel abandoned and it brings with it a martyr spirit that makes you think you have to do it all.
>
> "You two are willing to do the hard work. Stop regretting the problem and start rejoicing that there is a solution. If you use the fact that there is a problem to control your circumstances, your circumstances will control you. That is hope deferred."

The Lord told us about Barbara's god:

> "I challenge your thinking that says, 'Unless I push, nothing happens.' That makes you god of your own world. So even when you pray and acknowledge Me, it is all subordinate to your belief that you must bring everything to pass yourself.
>
> "Don't struggle under the weight of trying to take My place. You're carrying burdens I never intended for you.
>
> "When you stop, you will see a multitude of benefits. Pain will abate. Strength will return because you spend your energy wisely. Family relationships will improve. Personal fears will decline dramatically. Peace and joy will take their place."

Character is the currency of heaven. That is why man's time on Earth is intended for him to become spiritually mature. The Lord has emphasized to us the importance of being like Him and not blaming.

Reflections

The Lord told us Blaming Produces Stress...

"Pray for wisdom so you can get past determining fault and discover true grace toward one another.

"Whether you blame someone else or yourself, it creates stress, and stress is the enemy. You have to give up the right to blame if you're serious about resting in Me.

"Self-justification is evidence of stress. You would not defend yourself unless you felt victimized. And when you feel like a victim, your emotions prevent you from identifying your true oppressor, the devil. So you start blaming the people closest to you because they have the most input in your life. That produces more stress.

"Blaming comes from an attitude of entitlement. It makes you feel bad about yourself, and you feel alone. It is an enemy of teamwork. It is refusing to esteem others' gifts. And when they protest, you perceive it as a denial of your worth, and you become angry.

"When you are angry, you start condemning yourself when you run out of other people to blame, because it seems like a righteous thing to do. In fact, it is gross self-pity, and you always take self-pity out on other people. They don't buy into your condemnation because they love you too much to enable you.

"Anger is childish, foolish and very harmful. It serves no good purpose. It lies to you by claiming to be an expedient way to get things done, but it keeps you from accomplishing what you want to do. In fact, it makes you and those around you miserable. Like stress, anger is your enemy.

"You'll feel better when you learn to forsake anger. Your body reacts to how you think and feel. Imagine replacing anger with joy. What do you think that will do for your body? Joy brings healing if that's how you think in your heart, so be joyful instead of being angry and blaming."

Chapter 10 – Disciplining our Emotions

Reflections
The Lord told us about Accusing...

"After blaming often comes accusing. Accusing holds you back more than anything else. Judgment and self-righteousness accompany accusation, even if not expressed in words. It is demonizing people. The trap that goes with it is believing the other person is wrong, that you have nothing to apologize for, and there is no need for you to change.

"The enemy whispers that you are 'unappreciated,' 'exploited,' 'disrespected,' 'contradicted.' All these make you the victim. They anger you because the enemy makes you think it's all about you. When anyone you love is struggling and you are impacted, that doesn't mean their struggle is with you.

"This is one of the major avenues for stress that the enemy travels on. When you feel disrespected and unloved, the anger that rises up changes the chemistry of your whole being. This is one way the enemy steals, kills and destroys.

"Randy's self-pity and resentment have been exposed in this season. The symptoms have identified the disease, and now the medicine can be prescribed. The same holds true for you, daughter. Making everything about you greatly increases the likelihood of taking offense.

"It seems to you that the world is doing its business in spite of you or because of you, but never without you. You must learn not to see the results as your responsibility. Otherwise the world around you will look rebellious and ungrateful, and it will seem to be directed at you."

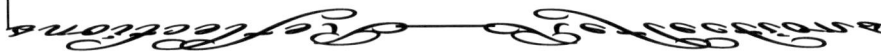

PRE-EXISTING ANGER

Anger turned outward is aggression; anger turned inward is depression.

Anger is not necessarily a response to circumstances. Often it is a pre-existing spirit, so what comes along that makes us angry is just the trigger, not the real cause. Anger was already there. That's why, when a person is habitually angry, little things set him off. His anger was looking for a reason to manifest.

Reflections

The Lord told us about Anger...

"If anger thinks you are onto its game, it will try to disguise itself. Anger may appear as impatience or indifference. It tries to remain by convincing you that you are right or entitled.

"Anger is a stubborn spirit. It uses your perception of the past as a legal right to remain. It convinces you that indulging yourself will make you feel better when, in fact, it produces more anger.

"Indulgence says, 'I must do this for myself because no one else will.' That is an expression of disappointment which comes from anger that is already there.

"Recognize anger as a spirit, not an emotion. It seems like a feeling because that is the level it attacks you on. The Bible describes God in one word – Love. It describes Satan as angry."

DISCOURAGEMENT

Part of disciplining our emotions is learning to overcome discouragement. Discouragement is intended to take away our future and our hope which God promises. It is a subtle form of unbelief and an attack from our adversary, who wants to weaken our faith by assailing our hope. It makes God angry at the enemy of our souls, not at us.

Reflections

The Lord told us about Complainers...

"Do you see many Christians as whiners and complainers? Do they blame others for their woes, and believe they are unfairly singled out for persecution?

"A lot more people believe this than it actually happens to because they see it as a mark of distinction and spirituality. If sorrow is all you see, sorrow is all you will have.

"Jesus talked about suffering for the sake of righteousness, so many people erroneously conclude that all unpleasantness proves their goodness. At the same time, they want to blame someone for it."

Reflections

The Lord told us about Anger and Offense...

"Once you are offended, it becomes easier and easier to take offense. Soon everyone offends you and you are miserable. The more you indulge offense, the longer it takes to get over it. Giving up the right to be offended will help you enjoy your day.

"Here's the first step: When you brood over offenses, you are murmuring in your mind, dwelling on complaints and lodging accusations. That just makes you angrier. Forgive and be free.

"Don't try to hold anyone hostage. As long as you look for people to blame, you are not free. When love covers a multitude of sins, it has no need to blame or take offense."

Basic Rules for Letting Go of an Offense

"1. It's the other person's problem. It's not your problem unless you make it your problem.

"2. Even though it sounds personal, don't take it personally.

"3. Don't add to the problem by prolonging it. If someone unloads on you, the more you say, the more the other person has to take issue with, and the longer it takes to get past it.

"4. Remember that the other person is not the source of your peace. Therefore, he can't take it from you unless you give it to him.

"5. When you are insulted and your character is impugned and your efforts at reconciliation are rejected, think of your crucifixion as mostly painless. Be glad that's all you have to suffer for the sake of your beliefs.

"6. When you learn not to interpret transgressions as personal, you will walk in forgiveness. It is not really the other person that transgresses against you. It is a spirit which wants to put him in bondage – and you too, if you let it."

Reflections

The Lord told us about His Anger...

"Where does My anger come from? When you think of anger over sin, you can easily see Me judging rebellion. But to know My love is to understand that I AM angry at what sin does to you and how you are duped into it.

"When you are deceived into unbelief and disobedience, the enemy is defrauding you. He knows most people are not disposed to sin willingly, so he tricks them into it. That makes Me angry.

"Cruelty makes Me angry. Disregard for the value of life and the land draws My anger. But what makes Me most angry is when people who know Me exercise the vanity of putting gods and idols ahead of Me. That breaks My heart because they are exchanging the truth of who I AM for a lie.

"I make Myself abundantly visible, yet people say they can't see Me. I AM beneficent (doing and producing good), yet people blame Me for evil. I AM the maximum expression of love, yet people believe I AM mean. This kind of deception stirs My wrath, not at the people taken in by it but at the deceiver."

PRAY Father, help me to love discipline. Thank You that Your discipline is for my good and advancement. It brings prosperity to my soul – my mind, personality and emotions.

Lord, remove what is dead in me (unproductive) and prune what remains to produce more fruit of goodness.

Differences Between Men and Women

Barbara: If we had only known that men and women were made to be different by God's design, we would have saved ourselves a lot of anguish. When I was young, my mother told me that little boys and little girls were basically the same; it was just how you brought them up. I found out that wasn't true when I had two sons and a daughter. They were totally different from birth, before I ever taught them anything. But I still believed the lie of boys and girls being alike until the Lord began to teach me.

I remember my friend standing in the kitchen with me, saying about her smiling husband, "Doesn't he see I need his help?" I thought, "He doesn't see, you have to tell him!"

Later the Lord showed me, "Women are angry over not being heard, respected and loved."

MEN HAVE TO BE TOLD

Waiting for my husband to catch up with me from another aisle in Walmart, I grabbed the first cart that came around the corner and said, "Stop!" When I looked up, it wasn't Randy. The other man, his wife and I laughed as she said, "He was obedient, wasn't he?" Men have to be told.

I watched a really funny video of a man explaining about men's and women's brains. Men think in separate boxes, he explained, and women's minds are like the Internet – everything is connected to everything else and laced with emotion. He said men don't really care that much. Women, who learn to be hypervigilant when they watch their children, don't miss a thing.

As I roared with laughter along with the audience in the video, the man explained about the "nothing" box that men prefer to go to most of the time. He quipped that nothing makes a woman more aggravated that when she sees a man doing nothing.

I even showed the video to my 14-year-old granddaughter to help her better understand her father and brother. She laughed too.

Although I laughed along with the audience, I learned a lot. That's how God made men and women. When we understand, we will be more tolerant and learn to laugh at ourselves.

SUGGESTIONS AND SUBMISSION

Randy: Many times, men see their wives' suggestions as nagging. Women generally have their husband's best interests at heart. I'm glad to have a helpmate who doesn't kowtow to the selfish doctrine of silent submission.

Before Paul wrote to the Ephesians that wives should submit to their husbands, he said to **"submit to one another in the fear of God"** (Ephesians 5:21 KJV). The Lord told Barbara and me to yield to whichever of us is more gifted in any situation. So I submit to her sometimes, and other times she submits to me, depending on who has greater wisdom for the need of the moment.

At one time we competed with each other a lot. It was the pride of self-sufficiency trying to replace humility and teamwork. There is no longer much competition or insecurity in our one-flesh relationship. We've learned how to live as the whole which is greater than the sum of its parts.

Barbara: I was feeling like Randy wasn't defending me to the kids, thinking that if my children knew he supported me, they would respect me. I suspected Randy of being passive again. The Lord said,

> "All women look like the bad guy. What makes you think you're any different? It's in My design that, as the spiritual heads of their households, men receive the most respect. It's in My design that, as nurturers and peacemakers, women receive the most love.
>
> "Don't fall into a defensive mind-set. Most of all, do not hold your husband up to derision. I chose him as your head to make you both the most you can be.
>
> "Trust Me with your husband. It's not your job to fix him but to help him. Learn the difference.
>
> "Daughter, you have to get rid of the attitude that no one can do anything right unless you tell them what to do. You see *big* because you want to get things done. It's hard to work together when you both want to be the boss.
>
> "Son, you see *small* because you deal in details. You have to get rid of the attitude that she is a nuisance. Don't fight over ownership; learn to cooperate.
>
> "Remember that the things you are least patient with in others are usually things you don't like about yourself."

Chapter 11 – Differences Between Men and Women

Reflections

The Lord told us about Listening...

"Why do women nag? Because they want to be heard. If a man's wife nags him, he might think he hears her but he is not listening.

"Nagging may not be due to something the husband does. For some women, it's just a bad habit. And for a few, it's a control issue. But mostly, it's a last resort to establish communication, even though it seldom works.

"So why don't men listen? It has to do with how they see the world differently than women do. Men are conquerors; women are protectors. Men look at the outside world as something to be tamed. Women see the world in terms of nurturing their children and sometimes other people. Men see the world in adversarial terms. Women see it in terms of available resources. Men want to overcome, and they appear to be undomesticated. Women are domestic and need sheltering.

"These differences don't have to work against each other, but they can be very distracting and impede teamwork. The man is always mastering something – opportunities at work, a fish in the water, or a golf ball on the green. He watches sports and pours his emotions into what other people are doing. He has two primary modes: work and play. Is it any wonder he is distracted while his wife tries to explain something?

"What about the woman? Her world seems inferior from man's point of view. She can be interpreted as little more than a cook, a maid and a baby-sitter. So when she has a good idea, the husband must release his stereotype and see her as an asset, not a servant.

"Even men who try to respect their wives have to battle the tendency to disregard their advice. For some, it is a problem: 'No woman is going to tell me what to do.' So women often have to prove themselves, and that can take a long time.

"Some women are rebellious. But generally, women want to please their husbands and help them. If men only knew that I see being open to their wives as a test of their humility before Me, they would cultivate their ability to listen."

GOD'S PLAN FOR HUSBANDS AND WIVES

Randy: My attitude toward Barbara used to be, "Don't lecture me, I know better than you do." I was resentful when she told me what to do, what to say and how to think. I interpreted being corrected as being contradicted and judged.

With time and humility, I have recognized how she sees what I miss and thinks of things from a different perspective that balances my outlook. She keeps me from doing foolish things, and saves me embarrassment. She helps me succeed in life. This is God's plan for husbands and wives.

Barbara: We were recently with some women who needed to be set free from having suffered childhood abuse and incest. Unfortunately, we find this to be way too common.

Reflections
The Lord told us about Respect...

"Daughter, trusting includes showing respect. That will always be hard in any area where you depend on a man ahead of Me.

"You have had difficulty respecting men. Any male infraction becomes a battle cry. Your issue with men is when they don't do what they are supposed to do. You are inadequate to make this judgment, so it boils down to their not doing what you expect them to do. That's how you know you have made them your source.

"These disappointments have fashioned an attitude. You are not unique in this, but I want you to learn wisdom from it. Otherwise you will never feel protected and loved, and your husband will never feel respected.

"You are imputing pride on men as a gender. Stop and consider it from another point of view. Women are overcomers where wisdom is concerned, and spiritual discernment, compassion and nurturing. Men are overcomers where adversaries are concerned.

"To most men, a mechanical malfunction immediately becomes an adversary. Women are not required to understand this. But when you judge it as pride, it takes pride to judge it. It is impatience judging impatience.

"By wisdom and humility, you can solve every problem. Wisdom is asking Me; humility is being like Me. "

Chapter 11 – Differences Between Men and Women

The Lord said, "Needing to be set free is not just for women who were sexually abused as children. It is for women who have father-hunger and unreturned love, which makes them feel unlovable."

I want my life to help other women. I want to be a living demonstration that the power of God helps us overcome every situation, and redeem every bad experience. I want to help other women not get stuck the way I was.

Men have also confided to us about experiencing these things which can keep people in bondage all their lives. The Lord showed us people who carry this baggage as going to their mailbox and finding hate letters they have written to themselves. That becomes their self-image, and they are subconsciously self-destructing. This is how the enemy gets people to surrender their lives to him, even while they try to follow Christ.

Reflections

The Lord told us about God-fearing Men...

"Husbands generally see their houses as a rest stop. Women generally see their houses as a showcase. There is a lot of no man's land between these two visions.

"You two share vision rather than compete with visions. You don't usually clash over the vision, only how to execute it. That makes you more of a team than in the majority of marriages.

"When it comes to spiritual matters, many men are intimidated so they are passive. Even if they have a godly foundation, they never really grow. There are a few who are seekers and desire My Kingdom. But in your country, a lot of men leave spiritual matters up to their wives.

"It's true that if Satan can get the man, he can get the whole family. America is proof. But America is not hopeless because America has a godly legacy.

"What do you think will happen when I get ahold of the men and raise up natural and spiritual fathers?

"The next appearance of Elijah is drawing near. Some can see it already. Pray for the hearts of the fathers to be restored and turned toward their families. There will be a lot less contentious women when there are a lot more God-fearing men."

PRAY Father, thank You for making me different and a complement to my spouse. Teach us how to appreciate our differences, and how to make better use of them to accomplish more good in our families and in the world. Help us honor and celebrate our differences to show forth the fullness of Your love.

God's Desires for Marriage

Marriage is a sacred agreement, a covenant not just between spouses but between them and God.

Marriage partners give up personal privileges in order to benefit each other, just as Jesus died to provide a covenant relationship between mankind and God.

Marriage is a mirror image of the relationship God wants to have with people.

Marriage is about –
- accountability
- intimacy
- honesty
- faithfulness

Marriage is intended to demonstrate to the world the relationship God wants with all people.

Marriage develops character, which includes –
- generosity
- humility
- unselfishness
- thoughtfulness

Marriage should mirror what a relationship with God is like. It reflects God's love toward every man.

 The Mirror Image Principle

"Your relationship with your spouse is a mirror image of your relationship with God. If you're having a problem in your marriage, don't look at your spouse, look at yourself. Get your relationship right with God and He will take care of your spouse."

How you treat your spouse is also how you're acting toward God. If your marriage is unhappy, don't accuse your spouse – examine yourself. Don't focus on how your spouse is behaving. Get your own attitude right toward God and He will correct your spouse.

Being in Agreement

Do you know that God sees a husband and wife as one flesh? *"For this reason a man shall leave his father and mother and be joined to his wife, and the two shall become* **one flesh**; *so then they are no longer two, but* **one flesh**" (Mark 10:7-8).

When two people who are one flesh don't agree, that couple is **double-minded**.

The Bible says a double-minded man is like a wave on the sea, driven and tossed by the wind. He is unstable in all his ways and should not think he will receive anything from God (James 1:5-8).

- Do you and your spouse disagree, argue and fight often?
- Is your marriage stable or does it feel like a storm?
- Does it seem like God does not hear your prayers?

"Husbands, in the same way be considerate as you live with your wives, and treat them with respect as the weaker partner and as heirs with you of the gracious gift of life, **so that nothing will hinder your prayers**" (I Peter 3:7).

 The Double-minded Principle

"Don't you know God sees married couples as one flesh? So if you disagree, you are like the double-minded man who will receive nothing from God."

Does your marriage need God's help? If you want a marriage that works, you must be willing to work at it God's way.

Teamwork is the answer. To become a team, a husband and wife must learn to come into agreement. Agreeing can be hard work, but it's worth it to have a happy marriage and a peaceful home.

Friends or Adversaries?

When you fight and argue often, it is a sign of competition. Such division keeps you from working together. Competition is the opposite of teamwork and unity.

*"Every kingdom divided against itself will be ruined, and every city or **household divided** against itself will not stand"* (Matthew 12:25).

"Walk worthy of the calling with which you were called, with all lowliness and gentleness, with patience, bearing with one another in love, endeavoring to keep the unity of the Spirit in the bond of peace" (Ephesians 4:1-3).

 ## The Spirit of Competition

"If winning an argument is more important to you than hearing your spouse, it is because you want to get your way at any cost – even your marriage."

Remember when you were dating and wanted to spend all your time together? Are things different now? Do you easily provoke each other to anger? Is your time frequently spent quarreling? Are you convinced it's your spouse's fault? Don't be so sure. Maybe you both have selfish ambition.

Arguing comes from pride, usually on the part of both people. If your home life seems like a contest for control, consider what you're contributing to the situation.

"If you are bitterly jealous and there is selfish ambition in your heart, don't cover up the truth with boasting and lying. For jealousy and selfishness are not God's kind of wisdom. Such things are earthly, unspiritual, and demonic. For wherever there is jealousy and selfish ambition, there you will find disorder and evil of every kind" (James 3:14-16).

Generous or Selfish Love?

Falling in love is easy; learning to love is hard. Love is much more than an emotional or physical feeling. Love is generosity, thoughtfulness and humility. Love makes sacrifices.

The wedding vow is a sacred promise to love, honor and cherish each other. Generous love wants the best for your spouse, often putting their needs ahead of your own. But when you are selfish, you focus on how your spouse can please you.

 ## Emotional Adultery

"If you are in love with the person you wish your spouse to be and not who your spouse is, that's emotional adultery."

Do you ever think you'd love your spouse more if he or she changed? That's emotional adultery.

Some forms of emotional adultery occur when we devote too much time and too much of ourselves to other things instead of our spouse – like a job, friends, relatives, children, a ministry, even church.

Emotional adultery requires repentance just as much as physical adultery. When you repent, ask for God's grace – not just that He will change your spouse but that He will change your heart.

"Love suffers long and is kind; love does not envy; love does not parade itself, is not puffed up; does not behave rudely, does not seek its own, is not provoked, thinks no evil; does not rejoice in iniquity, but rejoices in the truth; bears all things, believes all things, hopes all things, endures all things. Love never fails" (I Corinthians 13:4-8).

God's Gift to You

Marriage is God's wonderful gift to men and women, and He blesses it when they obey His principles.

"Godliness with contentment is great gain" (I Timothy 6:6).

"Be thankful in all circumstances, for this is God's will for you who belong to Christ Jesus" (I Thessalonians 5:18).

Before you can prosper in your marriage, you must first learn to be content and grateful. If you complain, God may take away your blessings, just as a good parent would do with an unruly child. The only time God grants the request of a complainer is to punish him with his own desires.

"Each man must love his wife as he loves himself, and the wife must respect her husband" (Ephesians 5:33).

A husband is accountable to God for what happens in his household. He is to love his wife by understanding her needs (which are different from his), honor her before the children and others, be sensitive in the areas where she is weaker, and provide a humble example of godly leadership.

A wife is to respect her husband, encourage him and to be his helper. Both spouses are to submit to and support each other, demonstrating the kind of love and relationship God wants to have with everyone.

 ## Good and Perfect Gift

"Your spouse is God's good and perfect gift to you. Therefore, when you complain against your spouse, you are complaining against God."

"Every good gift and every perfect gift is from above, and comes down from the Father of lights" (James 1:17).

Honor Each Other

Some people criticize their spouses in public. Wives and husbands should honor each other and not find fault with each other in front of other people, not even privately to your friends.

If a woman spends too much time in church while ignoring the needs of her husband, she is dishonoring him. Even asking friends to pray for her husband, if it is not done out of love and respect, can shame him and drive him away from the Lord.

In spiritual matters, a woman first should respectfully seek her husband's opinion, which draws them both closer to the Lord. Honoring your husband in this way can make him want to find the answer for both of you.

When wives seek other people's advice – even that of their pastors – it can be interpreted as saying, "My husband is not spiritual enough to know this so I must come to you."

Can you care about the soul of your spouse more than your own feelings? That's what happens when men love their wives and women respect their husbands.

 Ask Your Husbands at Home

"Wives, when you value your husband's opinion, you are honoring and respecting him – and respecting God, too."

"If [women] desire to learn anything, let them **ask their own husbands at home**…"(I Corinthians 14:35).

Listen to Your Helper

"Then the Lord God said, 'It is not good for the man to be alone. I will make a helper who is just right for him'" (Genesis 2:18).

Men don't do well alone. Married men live longer, healthier and more prosperous lives than single ones.

The original word for "woman" in the Bible means "helper." It comes from the same word used for the Holy Spirit. Jesus told His disciples—

"But the Helper, the Holy Spirit, whom the Father will send in My name, He will teach you all things, and bring to your remembrance all things that I said to you" (John 14:26).

Wives often have excellent spiritual discernment – the God-given gift of knowing the origin of a spirit. Wives should be their husband's confidants and counselors. Husbands can learn a lot from their wives. This is why Proverbs 18:22 says—

"He who finds a wife finds a good thing, and obtains favor from the Lord."

 If a Man Doesn't Listen...

"If a man doesn't listen to his wife, he won't listen to God, either."

Willingness to listen to others is a sign of humility. A man who can listen is a man who can learn. God wants to teach us the principles of His Kingdom. They are the opposite of how things are done in the world and cannot be understood without the help of God's Spirit.

Men are naturally proud. It takes a humble man to listen to his wife. Such a man is able to listen to God, too.

What is True Intimacy?

God not only wants us to be His children but also His intimate friends. Likewise, a marriage is about intimacy which begins with our emotional and spiritual nature. Physical intimacy without emotional and spiritual togetherness is empty. When couples agree emotionally and spiritually, they experience physical intimacy that is both satisfying and fulfilling.

A woman needs to be cherished, loved and listened to. She is an equal partner in the marriage relationship. God made women so men would have the benefit of their wisdom.

Men, your wife should be your best friend, your trusted confidant. God has given her to you to be a helper, counselor and best friend. If this is not happening, then you need to examine your relationship with God. Remember, **your relationship with your spouse is a mirror image of your relationhisp with God.**

Intimacy is more than a physical relationship. When there is a lack of intimacy with your spouse, check to make sure there is true intimacy with God. Be as open with your spouse as God would have you be with Him, and share your inmost thoughts, desires, hopes, fears, troubles and failures.

If you trust God and find joy in Him, you will be attached in the same way to your spouse. This is what the Bible calls "cleaving."

Before there were any children or parents on Earth, God told Adam and Eve in Genesus 2:24—

"Therefore shall a man leave his father and his mother, and shall cleave unto his wife: and they shall be one flesh."

This is God's pattern, both for marriage and our relationship with Him. He desires true intimacy.

Questions People Ask

Can you fall out of love?

Many people get married in the heat of passion. After they've been married awhile, most couples go through an adjustment time and that heat dies down. That's when a marriage has to be more than a matter of physical attraction. It's important to recognize marriage as a covenant made with God, not just each other. An exciting lifetime together is built on a shared vision and God's purpose.

What about divorce?

Divorce is selfishness. When people feel free to divorce, they are more concerned with getting their way than doing things God's way. Many things can give rise to divorce: impatience, envy, criticism, lust, depression – and all these are forms of self-centeredness. As soon as the relationship gets tough, people who divorce want to take the easy way out. Even in the worst of circumstances, trusting God can bring peace, healing and newness of life.

What if the spouse is immoral?

The woman usually wants a close relationship in her marriage. Deep inside, a man wants a godly marriage also. If either is unwilling to yield their heart to God, they are a target for many spirits of immorality. Through prayer, God can change the immoral or adulterous heart and produce fruit of humility, faithfulness and tenderness.

What if your spouse is abusive?

God doesn't want His children to suffer needlessly. He doesn't want them to lose their lives, their health or their security. But He also doesn't want them to leave due to discontentment and label it abuse. Usually it is a situation for which both spouses are responsible. Most divorces don't result from abuse but selfishness.

Why does God hate divorce?

Because He loves us, God hates whatever is not good for us, including divorce. Marriage is a covenant which most people make in Gods name. To break a marriage covenant is to take God's name in vain.

Is there a spirit of divorce?

No, there is selfishness. Divorce is a result of a deeper problem. Those who are selfish in their marriage should be told that divorce is not the easy solution.

Is divorce forgivable?

Yes. When you ask God, He forgives divorce. Those who have been forgiven for divorce should not feel guilty.

What if I think it's my spouse's fault?

Those who are quick to blame all their problems on their spouse should pray:

"Lord, start with me. Make me an example of godliness that my spouse cannot resist. Comfort me in my suffering, help me to keep my eyes on You, and increase my faith until I believe for a day when hurt will be replaced by joy, estrangement by faithfulness, and indifference by testimony. Father, let my life glorify You and let others be drawn to Your light in me. Teach me humility. Help me to control my tongue. Make me careful in my thought life. And cleanse my spirit. Amen."

 All Things Are Possible

You may think there is no hope for your marriage but through prayer things can turn around.

Jesus said, "With man this is impossible, but with God all things are possible" (Matthew 19:26).

SHILOH MINISTRIES BOOKS

MARRIAGE GOD'S WAY

God rescued our marriage by teaching us *The Mirror Image Principle*: "Your relationship with your spouse is a mirror image of your relationship with Me." This book is filled with things the Lord told us on how to strengthen marriage and faith.

$12 each *(includes shipping)*

MAKE THEM REMEMBER YOUR NAME

The inspirational life of Lt. Col. Kenny Cox (USA Ret.), who was decorated for valor after rescuing many people at the Pentagon on 9/11.

$12 each *(includes shipping)*

Things Hoped For Prayers & Declarations

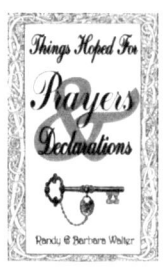

Encouraging and effective prayers, organized by topics. Easy to carry with you and use.

$10 each *(includes shipping)*

Make Room for Joy

The latest booklet in our *Timeless Wisdom* series.

$5 each *(includes shipping)*

Name Your Gates & Take Back Your Cities

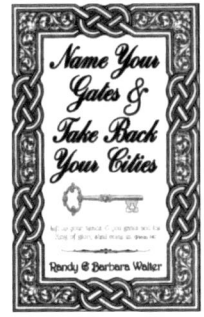

Applying these God-given tools is helping people transform cities and take territory.

$12 each *(includes shipping)*

The Rehearsal

Where Do You Hurt? Where Do You Hide?

These books free people from fear and shame to walk in God's destiny for their lives.

$10 apiece • $15 for both *(includes shipping)*

Things Hoped For

25 years of prophetic wisdom – Barbara's stories and adventures, Randy's teachings and revelations. Readers call it *"the most profoundly faith-building book I ever read"* • *"delightfully refreshing, enlightening, and very sobering"* • *"an honest portrayal of the walk of faith."*

$15 each *(includes shipping)*

Timeless Wisdom

Powerful messages from the Lord on *Kingdom Living, Prosperous Living* and *Revival Living*.

Set of 3 for $10 *(includes shipping)*

Send check and mailing address to: **Shiloh Ministries • 209 West St. Berlin, Maryland 21811** • ThingsHopedFor@comcast.net

THINGS TO DO
To Make Your Marriage Better

* Tell your spouse, **"I LOVE YOU"**...

   OFTEN

   EVERY DAY

   RIGHT NOW

* Make a list of 10 things you *LOVE* about your spouse.

* Read the list to your spouse.

* Enjoy each other's compliments.

* Realize how much you really love each other.

* Share the joy of being in love.

Randy & Barbara Walter
Shiloh Ministries
209 West St., Berlin, Maryland 21811
410-641-3953
shilohministries@comcast.net